Working with ENGLISH PREPOSITIONS

Nelson   Diane Hall

Thomas Nelson and Sons Ltd
Nelson House   Mayfield Road
Walton-on-Thames   Surrey
KT12 5PL   UK

51 York Place
Edinburgh
EH1 3JD   UK

Thomas Nelson (Hong Kong) Ltd
Toppan Building 10/F
22A Westlands Road
Quarry Bay   Hong Kong

© Diane Hall 1986
First published by Thomas Nelson and Sons Ltd 1986
ISBN 0-17-555417-X

NPN 10 9 8 7

Illustration by Colin Lewis

Printed in Hong Kong

CONTENTS

INTRODUCTION

Working with English Prepositions is not a straightforward reference book: it introduces and practises prepositions in a very different way from traditional reference and practice books. It examines all common English prepositions, as well as less common ones. It is intended for intermediate-level students who already have some knowledge of English prepositions, but who have difficulty in using them correctly. The language level assumed throughout is mid-intermediate (pre-Cambridge First Certificate), but the book can also be used successfully by students with a higher language level.

Many students of English make the mistake of trying to translate English prepositions into their own language. This is never successful because most prepositions express more than one idea, and while one meaning of the preposition may translate, the others often do not. For example, the preposition *for* can express the concepts of duration, exchange, benefit and suitability (among others), each concept remaining separate. **Working with English Prepositions** treats prepositions as expressions of concept, not as purely grammatical forms.

Another difficulty often encountered by students is that prepositions are usually practised in meaningless contexts. **Working with English Prepositions** uses a variety of exercises, both traditional and innovative, to contextualise the various uses of each preposition.

One of the difficulties of producing a reference/practice book on prepositions is having to decide exactly at which point a preposition ceases to be just a preposition and becomes part of a verb combination, or even a phrasal verb. This book concentrates on prepositions only, but inevitably some 'verb + preposition' combinations, and some phrasal verbs have been included. Compound prepositional phrases (e.g. *apart from*, *in addition to*) have been included because, in most cases, they function solely as prepositions.

Working with English Prepositions can be used in a variety of ways: specific prepositions can be located by means of the index and practised alongside others similar to them in concept, or general concepts can be dealt with as a whole. There is no systematic progression through the book, but it is advisable to study the whole of any concept before going on to another, as the prepositions often overlap and are repeated within concepts, thereby consolidating what the students have learnt.

Working with English Prepositions can be used in the classroom or for self-study at home. For this reason there is a key with the answers to all of the closed exercises (those which have only one possible answer) and a comprehensive cross-referencing index.

SECTION ONE

MOVEMENT

This section is divided into four categories:

1	Upwards and downwards	*(vertical motion)*
2	Passing through	*(passage)*
3	Coming and going	*(direction)*
4	Catching up and dropping back	*(following/preceding)*

All the prepositions in this section express relationships between a moving object and its destination.

---

1 UPWARDS AND DOWNWARDS

down to   off   on   onto   up   up to

down (to)   Movement downwards

He was lucky he didn't break his neck when he fell so heavily down the stairs.

Movement southwards

You must be so bored on that Scottish island. Come down to London to see us sometime.

Drop in status/respect

The accountant went down the company scale rapidly when he was found cheating the company.

off   Movement from one surface to a lower one

The girls screamed as Michael Jackson came off the plane.

on(to)   Movement from one surface to a higher one

He stepped onto the bus just as it set off from the stop.

up (to)   Movement upwards

The cat ran up the tree when she heard the dog.

5

Movement northwards (or to the capital)

They travelled up to Paris from Bordeaux once every year.

Movement upwards socially

She came a long way up the social scale when she married the Greek millionaire.

NB **to** expresses destination

Set phrases

Go up/down the road.
Go up to/down to the shop/pub etc.
Get on/off a bicycle/bus/train etc. (but *get into/out of a car*)

EXERCISES

1   Fill in the gaps with a suitable preposition.

    a   Get . . . the bus! It's about to go.
    b   Jeffrey doesn't like life on the oil rigs in the North Sea, so he's coming back . . . south soon.
    c   It's amazing how quickly Janice moved . . . the company ladder once she stopped being a typist.
    d   The girls surrounded the singer as he stepped . . . the stage.
    e   The fresh air will help your chest if you come . . . my chalet in the Alps.
    f   It's difficult to get . . . a camel.
    g   After six weeks at Number One the record fell gradually . . . the pop charts.
    h   There's nothing nicer than watching snowflakes float gently . . . the ground.

2   Make sensible sentences with these phrases.

a) She broke her leg when she fell	i) up the Eiffel Tower tomorrow.
b) In June he's coming	ii) on the back of the bicycle.
c) Put this basket	iii) off the horse that she was riding.
d) He was heartbroken when his team went	iv) up to London to watch the tennis.
e) The car will roll	v) down to the second division.
f) Let's go	vi) down the hill if you don't use the handbrake.

3 Put the preposition into the correct place in the sentence.

a You'll be able to see the parade better if   **onto**
   you climb this wall.
b The climber lost his hold, but   **down**
   fortunately only slipped a few feet to a ledge.
c The Rolling Stones' new single has   **up**
   jumped the charts.
d Another tile has just fallen the roof.   **off**
e I'm just going the road to get some milk.   **down**
f The plant has climbed the top of the window.   **up to**

4 Choose which preposition each diagram represents.

a **down/off/onto**   b **down/up/off**   c **on/up to/off**

d **onto/up/down**   e **off/down/up to**   f **up/off/on**

5 Now write a sentence about each of the diagrams above, using
   the correct preposition.

---

2 PASSING THROUGH

across along by down past through up over

across   Go from one side to the other, usually on the surface

It took us more than two days to get <u>across</u> the desert.
but: *The man jumped <u>across</u> the stream.*

along   Pass the length of
They will pass along Oxford Street and finish in Hyde Park.

by   Pass beside/next to
We took the path which runs by the river.

Avoid someone/something (idiom)
*I don't know what I've done; she passed by me as though
I didn't exist.*

down (up)   The length of
She walked up/down the road and didn't turn back.

past   Pass from one side to the other, laterally
I saw the shadow of a man run past my bedroom window.

through   Between the walls/parts of
I didn't think I'd get the car through that narrow entrance.

over   Go from one side to the other (similar to across, but usually abov
We flew over Switzerland on our way to Italy.

Set phrase *Pace up and down a room/cage/street etc.*

EXERCISES

1   Change this sentence according to the prompts.

For example: *The man ran across the bridge.*
Prompt: the tunnel
The man ran through the tunnel.

  a   the river bank
  b   the shops and the post office
  c   the promenade
  d   the alley
  e   the road several times
  f   the open field
  g   the policeman
  h   the road to the other side

2   Make sensible sentences from these phrases.

a) The lion paced
b) You can see their new TV
c) The express train thundered
d) Take the little road that runs
e) To reach the town centre, you pass
f) You should use zebra crossings to get

i)   through the gap in the curtains.
ii)   across busy streets.
iii) along the jagged coast.
iv) by the industrial estate.
v)   up and down the cage.
vi) past the station.

3   Complete these sentences.

a   You can take any of the bridges to get over . . .
b   Can't you sit down? It annoys me to see you pacing . . .
c   It only takes a few minutes to drive through . . .
d   I don't know anyone who can just walk by . . .
e   The bus route goes along the . . .
f   Didn't I see you walking past . . .
g   The smoke can only escape by going up . . .
h   To get to France from England you go across . . .

4   This is an aerial view of the route of a car rally. Describe the route that the competitors have to take, starting like this:

First, they have to go through the housing estate . . .

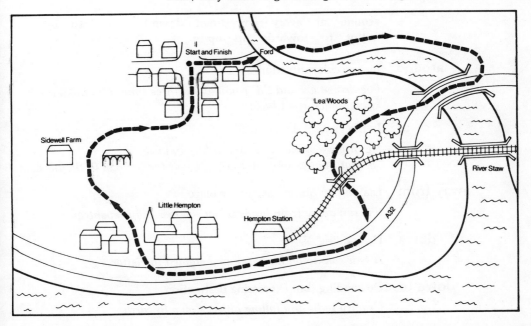

5 Write a sentence about each of these common road signs, using the preposition given.

a **through**   b **along**   c **up/down**

d **past**   e **over**   f **across**

3 DIRECTION

around   at   away from   down   down to   for   into   onto
out of   to   towards   up   up to

around   In a circular direction

I've driven around this roundabout three times and I still don't know which road I want!

at   In the general direction of

He threw a stone at me and it hit my knee.
"Is that man waving at you?" "No, at the woman in the fur coat."

away from   Leaving an object, person or place

She ran away from home when she was only seventeen.

down   Descending

A tear ran down his cheek and stained the letter.

down to   Descending, but expressing destination

Gravity pulls any falling object down to earth.

for   With a destination of
Columbus set sail for India in the late 15th century.

into   To a destination within something
The silent figure disappeared into the wood.

onto   To a destination on something
He put the open book onto the table and fell asleep.

out of   To a destination outside something
He shot out of the room as if the devil were chasing him.

to   In the specific direction of
To the airport, please. And hurry! My plane leaves very soon.
Could you give this record to Sally, please?

towards   In the general direction of
The tide crept slowly towards the sleeping figure on the beach.

up   Ascending
The burglar climbed up the pipe and forced the window open.

up to   Ascending, but expressing destination
You'll be able to reach if you climb up to the top of the stepladder.

Set phrases

Get away from it all
Come down to earth/reality etc.
Out of the frying pan, into the fire

NB   Compare

He shouted at me.   (He was angry.)
He shouted to me.   (He wanted to attract my attention.)

and also:

He threw the ball at me.   (He wanted to hit me with it.)
He threw the ball to me.   (He wanted to give it to me.)

EXERCISES

1   Choose the correct preposition.

   a   The hunter shot the deer as soon as it came — *out of/ from/around* — the wood.

   b   I'm upset because my best friend shouted — *to/towards/ at* — me this morning.

   c   You've just missed Ms Brownlow; she left — *for/to/into* — Greece this morning.

   d   The snowball became larger and larger as it rolled — *down to/up/down* — the hill.

   e   After a long, hard day I love getting — *onto/into/out of* — a hot bath.

   f   As the boxer realised he was getting — *at/away from/ towards* — the end of the round he started to relax.

2   Put these words into the correct order to make sensible sentences.

   a   need/ into/ the United States/ you/ a/ get/ to/ visa

   b   the/ away from/ ran/ summer camp/ brother and sister

   c   run/ leg/ I/ hurt/ couldn't/ my/ for/ the/ because/ bus/

   d   can't/ armchair/ get/ I/ this/ out of

   e   winner/ stage/ onto/ stepped/ the/ the

   f   gun/ aimed/ the/ at/ the/ was/ president

3   Look at the diagrams below and list the prepositions that each one illustrates.

For example:

into, onto

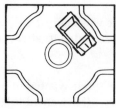

a

b

c

4   Now make sentences about the diagrams above, starting with the example.

5 A newspaper reporter made these notes during an interview with a famous singer, Alice Spring. Write the notes into full sentences, using the prepositions given.

away from	1 Left home 16
to	2 → San Francisco
around	3. Travelled SF → Los Angeles → New York → SF
to/for	4 Returned → LA. Then → Hollywood
up	5 Ambition—go ↑ film world
into	6 At 21 part of acting circle
out of	7 Soon took drugs, then rejected by acting world
out of	8 Disappeared—age 30— (clinic for alcoholics)
into	

4 CATCHING UP AND DROPPING BACK

after   ahead of   behind   in front of

after Following (pursuit)
The lamb ran playfully after its mother.

ahead of Preceding
The scout ran ahead of the body of the army to locate the enemy.

behind Following
You won't hear any of the guide's commentary if you lag so far behind the others.

in front of Preceding
Run on in front of me and ask the bus driver to wait.

EXERCISES

1 Fill in the gaps with a suitable preposition.

a Can't you walk a bit faster? You're always one step . . . me.

b I do have some good ideas, but somebody else is always . . . me.

c The dog chased . . . the stranger that threatened its territory.

d The car . . . mine braked very hard; I couldn't avoid hitting it.

e My watch is always three minutes . . . yours, that's why I never arrive late.

f He's now only two metres . . . his nearest challenger and is looking very tired.

g I started running when I heard someone running . . . me.

h When cars were first invented a man had to walk . . . each one waving a flag.

2 Make sensible sentences from these phrases.

a) The dog escaped and chased

b) Are you really keeping

c) I'll find it difficult if I drop

d) It's not the custom to walk

e) If I hadn't walked

f) The group of tourists entered the pyramids excitedly

i) ahead of the others in your field?

ii) in front of your wife here.

iii) after their guide.

iv) ahead of the guide, I wouldn't have fallen in the hole.

v) after the sheep.

vi) behind the others in my Italian class.

3 Put these words in the correct order to make sensible sentences.

a ducks/ behind/ mother/ baby/ swim/ always/ close/ their

b always/ ahead of/ thinking/ step/ me/ is/ your/ one

c behind/ frightened/ never/ horse/ a/ walk

d lost/ thief/ chased/ police/ but/ him/ the/ after/ the

e a few/ others/ steps/ winner/ in front of/ all the time/ the/ was/ the

f ahead of/ that/ Leonardo da Vinci/ people/ time/ say/ was/ his

4   Look at this diagram. It shows the final few seconds of a
marathon. The chart next to it should show the final order of
the runners. Read the commentary below and fill in the chart.

PLACES	
1	
2	
3	
4	
5	
6	

The leaders are now approaching the end of this year's
marathon. Ahead of the others is Gerald Ruskin, the Scotsman.
Louise Mitchell, the 1984 Ladies' World Champion, is doing
well but is finishing after the first five; just ahead of her is
Andrew Jameson and coming up behind Ruskin is Roy Davies,
this year's favourite, though he can't win now. Just after him
comes Mandy Selby, the veteran lady runner. And just in front
of Jameson is Chris Pride, the youngest official entrant.

CONSOLIDATION OF SECTION ONE

1   Fill the gaps with a suitable preposition.

a)   You walk so fast you're always five
steps . . . me.

b)   He's going . . . the Channel in a
bathtub, but a boat is going to sail
. . . him in case of emergency.

c)   You may go . . . the social ladder if
you marry this lord, but you'll soon
come . . . our level again if you
need us.

d)   The space shuttle takes off from
Cape Canaveral, goes . . . the
earth's atmosphere after a few
minutes, then flies . . . the earth
several times. Eventually it comes
back . . . the atmosphere and
comes . . . earth in California.

2   Complete these sentences.

a)   I can't focus properly if you're too
close. Move a little further away
from . . .

b)   I'm so terrified of flying that I'm
always very anxious to get off . . .

c)   He's one of the fastest runners this
country has got; he always finishes
a few paces ahead of . . .

d)   When the exam had finished the
students came out of . . .

e)   I wish I could stop my cats from
chasing after . . .

f)   If you'd like to go for a nice walk
we can take the path by . . .

g)   We haven't got time to queue for a
ticket. Let's just get on . . .

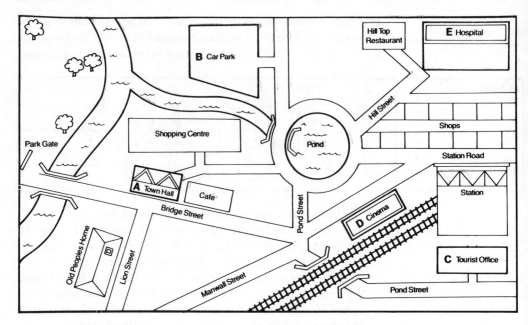

3 Look at the map and answer these questions.

For example: How do you get from **A** — the town hall — to the hospital? You go along Bridge Street, turn left into Pond Street, around the pond, across the little bridge, into Hill Street and up the hill.

a) How do you get from **A** to
   i) the park?
   ii) the tourist office?
b) How do you get from **B** to
   i) the station?
   ii) the shopping centre?
c) How do you get from **C** to
   i) the cinema?
   ii) the town hall?
d) How do you get from **D** to
   i) the park?
   ii) the car park?

e) How do you get from **E** to
   i) the tourist office?
   ii) the park?

4 Only one bus serves this town; it has to call at the town hall, the shopping centre, the station, the hospital, the tourist office and the old people's home (not necessarily in that order). Plan the best route for the bus.

5 Complete this dialogue by filling in B's part. B is standing at the entrance to the car park.

A Excuse me.
B
A I'm new to this town, can you tell me how to get to the tourist office?
B

16

A   Thank you. Oh, I need to go to a shop, too. Where can I find one?

B

A   Good. Is there anywhere to eat near here?

B

A   How do I get there from here?

B

A   Thank you, and is there a park here?

B

A   Oh, I see, and how do I get there from the restaurant?

B

A   Thank you very much. You've been a great help.

6   Fill in this crossword using the clues opposite. Each answer is a preposition.

ACROSS

1   He finished the race only a few metres . . . the winner.
4   Turn right and go . . . the roundabout.
6   It's the third time he's run . . . prison. (4, 4)
8   I saw a mouse run . . . the kitchen floor.
9   It takes a few minutes to drive . . . the St. Gotthard Tunnel.
10 It's unhygienic to let animals get . . . the table.
11 Greedy? As soon as we got to the party he made . . . the food table, without even saying 'hello' to the host.

DOWN

2   Get . . . bed this instant!
3   The car rolled backwards . . . the slope.
4   I can't help feeling that you're always one step . . . me. (5, 2)
5   I'm driving . . . Edinburgh, but I'm not going quite so far.
7   I must get . . . this boring town, even if it's only for one day. (3, 2)

SECTION TWO

POSITION

This section is divided into three categories:

1 One up, one down   *(superiority/inferiority)*
2 Close at hand   *(proximity)*
3 Before and behind   *(preceding/following/opposing)*

All the prepositions in this section express relationships between a stationary object or person and its or his position.

---

1 ONE UP, ONE DOWN

> above   after   below   beneath   down   on
> on top of   over   to   under(neath)   up

above Directly higher than something
The plane is now circling above New York.

Of higher rank or importance than someone/thing
In the Protestant hierarchy an Archbishop comes above all the other ministers.

Too good for someone/thing (idiom)
Don't play the fool. You should be above such childish games at your age.

after Slightly inferior to
His opinion is second only after the managing director's.

below Directly lower than something
There's a huge bruise on your leg, just below the knee.

Of lesser rank or importance than someone/thing
In a hospital a nurse comes below a sister, and a sister comes below a matron.

Not good enough for someone/thing (idiom)
Sweeping the streets is <u>below</u> me; I'd rather starve to death!

beneath As *below*, but archaic and used only in idiomatic phrases, such as the following:

<u>beneath</u> contempt, <u>beneath</u> one's notice, to marry <u>beneath</u> one

down At or in a lower part of
He lives further <u>down</u> the hill.

on As *above*, but with contact with the surface
There's a brilliant green parrot <u>on</u> his shoulder!

on top of As *on*, especially for height or emphasis
Put that case <u>on top of</u> the wardrobe, not in it!
He's standing <u>on top of</u> the building. I think he's going to jump!

over As *above*, but the object is closer
Have you seen the new bridge they've built <u>over</u> the river?

to Expressing relative subordinate rank
The deputy head is second only <u>to</u> the headmaster.

under As *below*, but the object is closer
In a few years there may be a tunnel <u>under</u> the English Channel.

underneath As *under* (less common, but not archaic)
It must be awful to work <u>underneath</u> the ground, like miners do.

up As *down*, but expressing the opposite
You can fish further <u>up</u> the river but not here.

Set phrases
<u>Above</u> suspicion
Downstream/upstream
Second <u>to</u> none

EXERCISES

1 Fill in the gaps with a suitable preposition.

   a The TV aerial will only work if you put it . . . the roof.

   b In many social systems the professions of doctor and lawyer are ranked . . . all others.

   c The countess isn't likely to marry the gardener; that would be marrying . . . her.

   d You can get stamps in the post office. It's only a few minutes' walk . . . the road.

   e If he speaks to me so rudely again, I shall simply refuse to have him . . . my roof.

   f Now I know why my rent is so cheap! There's a dancing class twice a week in the flat . . . mine.

   g The wreck of the famous ship, the *Mary Rose*, was . . . the sea for several hundred years.

   h Chris Lloyd is ranked second only . . . Navratilova in the tennis world.

2 Look at the sketch and then correct the sentences below it. The first one is done for you.

   a There's a church above the cliff.   *on top of*

   b Some people are sitting after the cliff.

   c A person is lying below the steps.

   d The boat is above the sea.

   e The swimmer is on top of the water.

   f The birds are on top of the cliff.

   g The person is sitting over the side of the boat.

3 Look at this list of the six best-selling car manufacturers in Britain, with their percentage (%) share of the UK market.

Ford — 27.14%
British Leyland — 18.89%
General Motors — 18.55%
Volkswagen-Audi — 5.65%
Nissan — 4.17%
Peugeot-Talbot — 4.14%

Now match the questions and the answers.

a Which manufacturer comes directly above Peugeot-Talbot on the list?
b Which one is top of the list?
c Which one comes after Volkswagen-Audi?
d Which one is second only to Ford?
e Which one comes below British Leyland?
f Which one is one place higher up the list than Nissan?

i) Nissan   ii) Volkswagen-Audi   iii) General Motors
iv) Ford   v) Nissan   vi) British Leyland

4 Paraphrase these sentences, using the preposition given.

a	In chess, a bishop is worth more than a knight.	**above**
b	In the last Eurovision Song Contest France came second and Spain came third.	**after**
c	He lives on the 5th floor. I live on the 4th floor.	**below**
d	The American Embassy building always flies the US national flag.	**over**
e	Your newspaper is under your book.	**on**
f	What he did is too cruel even to be despised.	**beneath**
g	You'll find more fish as you approach the river estuary.	**down**

5 This is a list of names and exam results. But they are mixed up. Complete the table by reading the paragraph below.

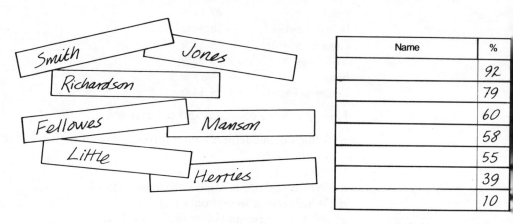

Name	%
	92
	79
	60
	58
	55
	39
	10

Richardson came first in the class. He came above all the others. Fellowes came above three students but also below three students. Herries came directly after Fellowes, and Jones came below all the others. Smith performed way beneath his usual standard, coming above only Jones. Manson was second after Richardson.

2   CLOSE AT HAND

against   along   alongside   around   at   beside   by
on the left/right of   near   next to   towards

against   To be directly touching something

I'll be very annoyed if I see your bicycle leaning against the rose tree again.

along   To be placed by the side of something

There are emergency telephones all along the motorway. I don't see how you could miss them.

alongside   To be in position next to something

The two horses ran alongside each other as they approached the finishing post.

around   Somewhere in the vicinity
I know there's a cafe around here somewhere.

at   Exact position
Wait for me right at the end of that narrow street.

Approximate position
He runs a stall at the market every Sunday.

beside   At the side of
The Rhine wines are produced mostly in vineyards beside the river.

by   In the region of
He lives in a pretty little cottage by the sea.

on the left/right of   Immediately next to on the left/right hand side
I was a bridesmaid at her wedding. In that picture I'm on the left of the bride.

near   In the vicinity of
I'd like to send him to this school because we live very near it.

next to   Very close, almost touching
We can't possibly buy the house next to the cemetery.

towards   Close to (idiom)
We're getting towards the end of the journey now.

*In appears in Section Six under *Inclusion*.

EXERCISES

1   Choose the correct preposition:
   a   Docks are usually built — *on the left of/at/by* — the coast.
   b   The guide met the tourists — *alongside/at/around* — the station.
   c   I parked the car — *alongside/around/towards* — your caravan.
   d   I spent the afternoon — *beside/alongside/against* — the river.

23

e You'll get covered in paint if you lean — *towards/against/ at* — that freshly-painted wall.

f The new cinema is in Bridge Street, — *around/on the left of/towards* — the service station.

g The Chancellor of the Exchequer lives at Number 11, Downing Street, — *alongside/around/next to* — the Prime Minister.

h I said he'd bought a new apartment — *towards/near/ around* — Paris, not in the town centre.

2 Look at this map of Brightchester and answer the following questions.

a Where is the cafe?
b Is the wine bar next to the bank?
c Where can you buy a newspaper?
d Where is the bank?
e Where is the chemist's in relation to the grocer's?
f If you are looking out of one of the offices, is the wine bar on the right of the restaurant?

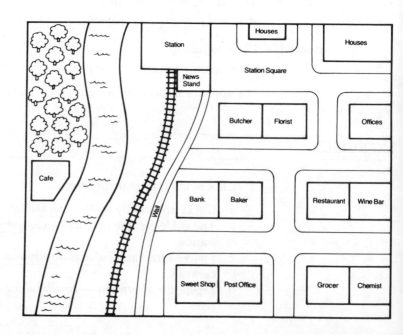

3 Now complete these sentences, still referring to the map.

    a   The railway line runs alongside . . .
    b   There are several houses around . . .
    c   There is a newspaper stand at . . .
    d   There are some trees by . . .
    e   The grocer's shop is next to . . .
    f   There is a baker's on the right . . .
    g   A wall has been built alongside . . .
    h   There is a very pretty cafe by . . .

4 Look at this plan of a bed-sitting room and complete this letter.

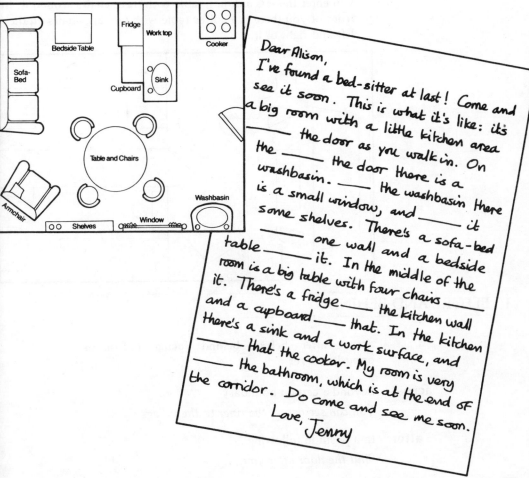

Dear Alison,

I've found a bed-sitter at last! Come and see it soon. This is what it's like: it's a big room with a little kitchen area _____ the door as you walk in. On the _____ the door there is a washbasin. _____ the washbasin there is a small window, and _____ it some shelves. There's a sofa-bed _____ one wall and a bedside table _____ it. In the middle of the room is a big table with four chairs _____ it. There's a fridge _____ the kitchen wall and a cupboard _____ that. In the kitchen there's a sink and a work surface, and _____ that the cooker. My room is very _____ the bathroom, which is at the end of the corridor. Do come and see me soon.

Love, Jenny

5 Read this description of a small flat and label the diagram.

Go in through the front door. The bathroom is on the left and the kitchen is on the right. In the bathroom there is an avocado bath along the wall, with a matching wash-basin by the window and a toilet next to the bath. The kitchen has work-surfaces along the wall opposite the door, with a sink. The fridge is on the right of these, under the window, the cooker on the left. The living room/bedroom is at the end of the hall. As you enter there is a large armchair on the left. Next to it there is a small cupboard. Along the wall under the window there is a large sofa-bed and on the right of the sofa, against the wall, there is a double wardrobe. On your right as you enter there is a dining-table with three chairs around it. In front of you there is a coffee table with two armchairs on the left and right of it.

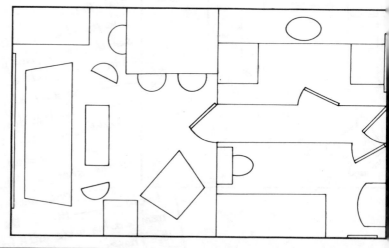

3 BEFORE AND BEHIND

across after before behind facing in front of
opposite over

across Beyond a certain boundary
You can see across the river to the village.

after In a position following
Shut the door after you.

before In a position preceding
The name should come before the address.

In the presence of
The thief will come before the magistrate tomorrow.

behind In a position further back
There's a squirrel behind you. Quick, turn round!

facing Looking towards something
I'd like a room facing the sea.

in front of In a position further forward
I get very nervous whenever I stand in front of an audience.

opposite Looking towards something (similar to *facing*)
I hope they don't build a block of flats opposite our house. It'd spoil the view.

over On the other side of
The post office is over the road from the grocer's.

EXERCISES

1 Change this sentence according to the prompts.

For example: *She stood behind her children.*
Prompt: the sea *She stood facing the sea.*

a the person talking to her
b the road
c the river
d the judge as he passed sentence on her

2 Fill in the gaps with a suitable preposition.

a The flat's wonderful, except for the bedroom, which is . . . the cemetery.
b I wish people would be more considerate when they park their cars and not leave them . . . my gate, blocking it.
c It's easy to get to the town from here; the bus stop is just . . . the road.

d Take the first turning . . . the traffic lights.

e The old lady stood . . . the door and when the burglar opened it she hit him with the vase.

f It's funny. Her office is directly . . . mine, but we've never met.

g The deserter had to appear . . . a military court.

h There's a natural border here; we're in Switzerland but . . . the river it's Germany.

3 Look at this plan of a shopping street.

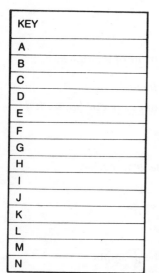

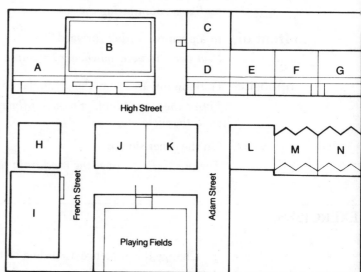

Now read the text below and fill in the key with the names of the shops.

In the High Street there is a record shop and a post office in front of the playing fields. The post office is directly opposite the large department store, Peter Lewis. Opposite the record shop, across Adam Street, there is a pet shop, facing which, from left to right (looking at the plan) there is a boutique, a bank, a dry cleaner's and a patisserie. Behind the boutique, facing the department store, there is a travel agent's. Directly across the High Street from the cleaner's and the patisserie are the town doctor's and dentist's surgeries respectively. Over French Street from the post office there is a small cafe and next to that the supermarket. Finally, the local employment exchange is opposite the cafe.

4 Make sensible sentences from these phrases.

a) Your signature comes
b) The soldiers can see each other
c) I'd like to sit
d) The only real problem is the building
e) The couple should stand
f) For being so naughty you can stand
g) Live badly now, but we all come
h) These secrets are kept

i) facing the wall for ten minutes.
ii) opposite the guest of honour.
iii) before our maker in the end.
iv) after mine, as I'm the main witness.
v) behind closed doors.
vi) in front of the school, which blocks out the sunlight.
vii) before the priest in the ceremony.
viii) over the Berlin Wall.

5 Use the prepositions in this unit to make sentences about the sketches.

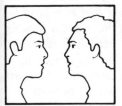  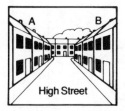 

a   The two men stood . . .

b   There are two bridges . . .

c   The Smiths (A) live . . . the Whites (B)

d   One girl sits . . . the other

CONSOLIDATION OF SECTION TWO

1 Choose the best preposition.

a) He jogged — *up/over/around* — the park three times before breakfast.

b) All root vegetables, such as potatoes, are grown — *under/above/at* — the ground.

c) Push all the furniture — *over/against/in front of* — the wall to make a dancing area.

d) The worst areas of towns are often — *along/near/facing* — the station.

e) The defendant comes — *before/towards/along* — the judge tomorrow.

f) You can't have missed the look on his face. He was sitting directly — *opposite/behind/on the left of* — you.

g) All the Picassos are hanging — *beside/along/across* — the south wall of the gallery.

h) Don't put flowers — *under/above/on top of* — a TV; the water can be dangerous if it's spilled.

29

2 Look at this plan of a restaurant, then fill in the gaps in the paragraph below with a suitable preposition.

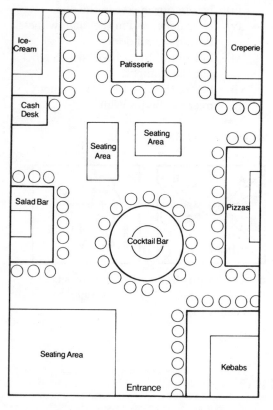

The New Eating Place — Somewhere new to eat! Different kinds of snack meals, all . . . one roof. On the . . . of the plan is a salad bar for hot, summer days and . . . it plenty of comfortable seating. . . . the salad bar there is a cocktail bar and directly . . . that a counter for pizzas and pasta. . . . that there is a kebab counter and . . . it a creperie. . . . the creperie there is a patisserie and finally an ice-cream bar just . . . the checkout. Extra seating is provided all . . . the bars.

3 Draw a simple sketch from this description. You will need a square piece of paper and a pencil.

Let's start at the top of the page. On the left of the picture there is a large hill which dominates most of the top; next to it on the right there's a much smaller hill. There are some birds flying around the top of the larger hill; it has trees all up the left-hand slope and a big building on top of it. Just beyond the smaller hill and on the right you can see the walls of an old castle. Now, in the middle of the picture there is a river that runs from the left to the right; the water is flowing to the right. On the left-hand side, near the river but just below the large hill, there is a farm with farmland all around it. A railway runs from the bottom of the large hill, across the river and into a station, which is in the centre of the picture. A road runs from in front of the station slightly to the right, over the river, then off to the left. Behind the station there are some houses and there are also some by the river, on the other side. Alongside the road, on its left, there are some trees (from the other side of the bridge to the end of the picture) and on the opposite side of the road there is a brick wall. In front of the river, to the right of the road, there is a large building, next to which, on the right, is a swimming pool. Finally, on the river, in front of the brick wall, just down from the bridge, you can see a small sailing boat.

Now compare your picture with those of your classmates.

4 Write a description of this house (on two floors), using the prepositions you have learnt in this section.

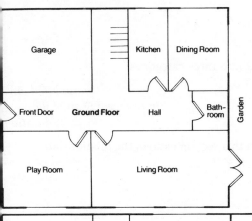

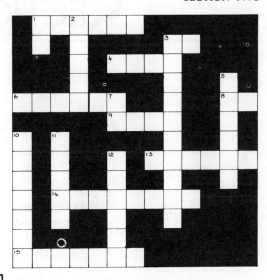

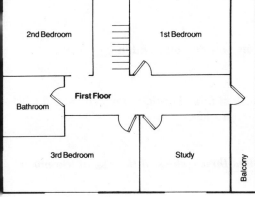

5 Fill in the crossword using the clues. Each answer is a preposition.

ACROSS

1 He appeared . . . the magistrate who fined him £50 for speeding.

3 You'd have to be further . . . the hill to see the view.

4 But further . . . the hill to escape the strong wind.

6 There's always a souvenir shop . . . any historical place. (4, 2)

8 We can have a drink . . . the airport.

9 We're going to stay in a hotel that's quite . . . the town but is still very quiet.

13 Is something happening . . . that door? I can hear people laughing.

14 I wish we didn't live . . . a football pitch.

15 Only another twenty miles, we're getting . . . the end of the motorway.

DOWN

1 I want to spend a few days . . . the sea.

2 Don't stand in . . . of me, I can't see a thing.

3 There's a lot of rust . . . the car.

5 It's a marvellous room with a window . . . the racecourse.

7 I hate being . . . a boat. I get seasick.

10 Don't rest that bicycle . . . the car, you'll scratch the paintwork.

11 We didn't get to sleep till three o'clock because the hotel disco was . . . our room.

12 There are a lot of garages . . . here, but they're all very expensive.

31

SECTION THREE

TIME

This section is divided into three categories:

1 At the moment   *(pinpointed time*
2 Then and now   *(time preceding and following*
3 How long?   *(duration*

All the prepositions in this section express the relationship between times and events. ʼ

---

1 AT THE MOMENT

about   around   at   in   inside   on   within

about Approximate time

The lecture should finish at four, but that's unlikely, so I'll meet you about 4.30 in the coffee bar.

around Approximate time

We should arrive around three o'clock, if there's not too much traffic.

at Exact time

The train leaves London at 8.30 am and reaches Edinburgh at 12.45 pm.

Occasions, special days

We usually have four days' holiday at Easter.

in Parts of a day, seasons and years

Very few shops are open in the evening.

inside Defined periods (As *within* but slightly more colloquial)

You don't think they'll finish building the new swimming pool inside a year, do you? Be realistic!

on   Names of days

The new teacher will start on Monday, 13 September.

within   Defined periods (rather formal)

I'll be back with the shopping within an hour.

Set phrases

In time (with time to spare)
On time (at the given time exactly)
On the dot (precisely)

EXERCISES

1   Change this sentence according to the prompts.

For example: *We expect the ambassador to arrive at 2.30 this afternoon.*

Prompt: evening

We expect the ambassador to arrive in the evening.

a   Monday
b   the next hour
c   four o'clock (approximately)
d   Easter
e   the weekend
f   May
g   time
h   10.30 tomorrow morning

2   Fill in the gaps with a suitable preposition.

a   Most British children go to school . . . the morning and . . . the afternoon.
b   The sales start . . . 2 January but all the best bargains disappear . . . the first few hours.
c   Don't rush to get there . . . time, the doors open . . . eight but the main film starts . . . nine.
d   The term will finish next summer . . . 29 June, so I'll go on holiday . . . the first week of July.
e   You can open your presents . . . Christmas Day, not before.
f   By Concorde it's now possible to fly to New York from Europe . . . four hours.
g   My mother's so sentimental. I hope she doesn't cry . . . my wedding next week.

33

3 Answer the following questions.

a When were you born?
b When do you usually go on holiday?
c What time do you usually get up in the morning?
d When did man first land on the moon?
e In which month do you have the most public holidays in your country?
f How quickly can you read an average novel?
g On which day do you usually do your shopping?
h When do people give each other presents in your country?
i In which season do you get the best weather in your country?
j Do you usually arrive late for interviews? (Start with 'No . . .')

4 Write sentences about these diagrams.

a The year begins . . .

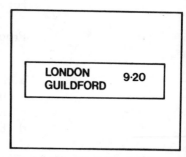

b The Guildford train leaves . . .

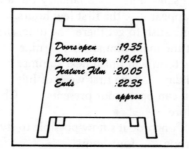

c The doors open . . .
The film . . .

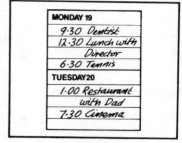

d On Monday . . .
On Tuesday . . .

5 Write these two telegrams in full.

Telegram

LIKE TO SEE YOU EASTER STOP ARRIVING SAT 6.30PM
STOP PHONE FRI EVE STOP

Telegram

SORRY NOT HOME APRIL STOP FREE APPROX END MARCH
STOP CAN YOU COME 25-26TH STOP

---

2 THEN AND NOW

after   before   by   past   to

after Following a time

*It's marvellous! All my lectures and seminars this year start after
nine.*

Following an event

'Did you manage to get to the station on time?'
'No, I got there ten minutes after the departure time, so I got a taxi.'

before Preceding a time

*Please try to arrive before eight o'clock or we'll miss the
beginning of the play.*

Preceding an event

Let's have a drink before dinner, and then we can eat.

by Preceding or at a time/point

*Give me your homework by Friday, then I can mark it at the
weekend.*

past Following a time (more colloquial than after)

There's no point in going to the party now, it's past midnight.

Telling the time

Doesn't time fly when you're having fun? It's half-past eleven already.

to Telling the time

'*What time is it?*'
'*It's already a quarter to six, let's go home.*'

NB   American English uses *after*, not *past*, when telling the time,
for example: *It's ten after six.* (And sometimes *before* instead of *to*

EXERCISES

1 Choose the correct preposition.

a The committee will discuss this question on Friday, so
please submit any suggestions — *by/before/after* —
Thursday.

b You've missed the last bus, it's already — *to/after/by* —
11.30.

c Last drinks! It's already — *past/to/by* — eleven and I've
got to close.

d We don't have to leave yet, the bus goes at ten and it's
only twenty — *to/before/past* — ten now.

e My father's dead, actually. He died a year — *before/after/
past* — my birth.

f It's Monday today, and I can keep my library books
another three days so I have to return them — *after/
before/by* — Thursday.

g Street lights are usually turned on just — *to/after/before*
— dark.

2 Paraphrase these sentences, using the preposition given.

a The time is one-fifteen.   **past**
b I must pay the deposit before or on Saturday.   **by**
c The concert begins at 10.45 and finishes   **to/past**
at 12.30.
d The train left at 10.50, but unfortunately   **to/past**
I got to the station at 11.05.
e She finishes at the office at six and then   **after**
she'll come and see you immediately.
f Ten-thirty is too late to arrive.   **before**

3   Match the watch-faces to the sentences and fill in the gaps
    with suitable prepositions.

a   It's half- . . . eleven.
b   It's twenty . . . three . . . the morning.
c   It's five . . . nine . . . the evening.
d   It's a quarter . . . three.
e   It's a quarter . . . one.
f   It's thirty minutes . . . midnight.
g   It's twenty-five . . . seven.
h   It's ten . . . two . . . the afternoon.

4   Look at this flight information board.

DEPARTURES			ARRIVALS		
8.55			9.05	LT079	FRANKFURT
9.10	AC1525	MONTREAL	9.10	AF1062	PARIS-CDG
9.15	DA729	MADRID	9.25		
9.30	PA1921	NEW YORK	9.30	BA9192	JOHANNESBURG
9.35	LT200	FRANKFURT	9.35	DA738	MUNICH
9.45	DA1910	MILAN	9.55	AA0107	TANGIER
9.50	PA8310	MONTEVIDEO	10.10		
10.10			10.15		
10.20			10.25	DA661	ATHENS

Fill in the missing flights above from the information in this
paragraph.

Only one flight leaves the airport before nine o'clock in the
morning, the BC218 to Edinburgh. Two flights leave after ten:
at ten past the AF1063 to Paris — Charles de Gaulle, and ten
minutes after that the SAS202 to Stockholm. There are three
arrivals from America in the morning: the first one arriving
from Miami at twenty-five past nine (BA4242); there's an
arrival from New York at ten-fifteen (PA1918) and five
minutes before that the PA2190 from Dallas.

5 Now answer these question with full sentences.

a How many departures are there before ten o'clock in the morning?

b How many flights arrive from Europe after 9.30, but before 10.30?

c If passengers have to arrive at the airport one hour before departure, by what time should you check in for your flight to Frankfurt?

d If you're meeting a friend from Munich, what time should you be at the airport? (Use *before*.)

e What time should you arrive at the airport if you want to fly to Sweden?

f Robert wanted to fly to Canada, but he arrived ten minutes after his flight had taken off. What time did he arrive?

g If it takes 45 minutes to fly to this airport from Paris, did Flight AF1062 leave Paris before or after 8.30?

h The plane coming from Paris returns to Paris soon after its arrival. How soon after?

3 DURATION

about   as from/of   between   during   for
from . . . till/until/up to   since   throughout
till/until   up to   within

about   Approximate duration

The carnival lasts about eight days.

as from/of   Unknown duration from a given time

The seat belt law will be in force as from 31 January.
As of today I won't eat any more cakes or chocolate.

between   From one point to another

The period between the two world wars was a period of depression for most of Europe.

during   Period of time

The weather was fantastic during our holiday; we were able to go onto the beach every day.

Event in a certain period
John Lennon was shot <u>during</u> an early morning walk.

for   Duration of a given length
In 1972 India had been independent <u>for</u> 25 years.

from . . . till   Duration between two given points
<u>From</u> the day he read the article on lung cancer <u>till</u> the day he died,. he didn't touch another cigarette.
(*Until* and *up to* are used in the same way.)

in   Specified duration
Wait for me here, please. I'll be back <u>in</u> a few minutes.

since   Duration from a given point until the present
India has been independent <u>since</u> 1947.

throughout   From the beginning to the end
<u>Throughout</u> her life, Golda Meir dedicated herself to the establishment of a Jewish state.

till   Duration to a given point
She'll be studying <u>till</u> 1985, when she takes her final exams.

until   Same as *till*

up to   Same as *till*

within   Specified duration
He'll have the solution <u>within</u> a few hours.

EXERCISES

1   Fill in the gaps with a suitable preposition.

   a   The French Revolution started . . . the reign of Louis XVI.
   b   The plumber will be here . . . two o'clock . . . five this afternoon.
   c   I was so terrified that I trembled . . . the whole trip.
   d   Gandhi lived in South Africa . . . many years.
   e   'Will you be long?'
      'No, only. . . another half an hour.'

f Mrs Young will be responsible for the department . . . next Wednesday.

g I haven't visited Morocco . . . I saw my cousin in 1975.

h Don't worry about me; the bus will get me home . . . an hour.

i Geologists believe Britain's coal resources will have run out . . . fifty years.

2 Make sensible sentences from these phrases.

a) He will be our new boss
b) A British Prime Minister stays in office
c) Britain has had four TV channels
d) Inflation in Britain dropped
e) Karl Marx lived in London
f) Luther King was assassinated

i) during 1984.
ii) from 1849 until he died in 1883.
iii) since November, 1982.
iv) for about five years.
v) during a strike by sanitation workers.
vi) as from 1 March.

3 Put these words into the correct order to make sensible sentences.

a I'll/ to school/ I'm/ go/ until/ 16/ have to
b he/ in/ for/ China/ stayed/ two years
c welfare officer/ to/ the/ between/ one/ report/ and five pm
d risen/ the/ few/ inflation/ during/ years/ has/ past
e in power/ about/ they've/ years/ been/ two/ for
f since/ my childhood/ been/ there / haven't/ I

4 Paraphrase these sentences, using the prepositions given.

a Because of a serious accident Elena was unable to walk between the ages of eight and thirteen.   from . . . to

b Martin has been living in Holland since 1979. It's now 1985.   for

c If they are lucky, African children spend approximately six years in full-time education.   about

d He proposed to his fiancee on a liner cruising the Mediterranean.   during

e I'm going to give up drinking. Today I'll have my last glass of wine.   as from

f He spent the whole of 1967 in prison.   throughout

5   Look at the chart below.

DOMESTIC HEATING METHODS
IN BRITAIN 1945-1980

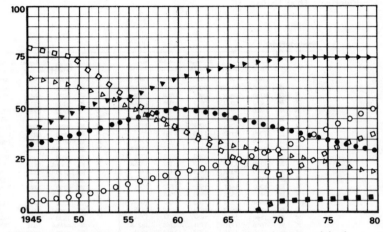

O CENTRAL HEATING
□ OPEN FIRES (SOLID FUEL)
▲ GAS
● ELECTRICITY
■ SOLAR HEATING
△ OIL/PARAFFIN STOVES

Write a few sentences about the success of each type of fuel, using prepositions of duration, like this:

Oil/paraffin heating

During the period from 1945 to 1980 the number of households using oil and paraffin fell greatly. In 1945 approximately 65% of all households were heated by this method, but by 1960 fewer than 50% were using it. From 1945 to 1960 the percentage dropped gradually, but between 1960 and 1980 it dropped a lot more quickly.

CONSOLIDATION OF SECTION THREE

1   Look at these sentences.

a)   He'll be here by Thursday.
b)   He'll be here within a week.
c)   He'll be here till the middle of the week.
d)   He'll be here till the weekend.
e)   He'll be here during the week.
f)   He'll be here till past midnight.
g)   He's been here since last week.

Now look at the phrases on the right. Each one of them can be substituted for one of the time phrases in the sentences on the left. Which one can go into which sentence?

i)   . . . from Monday to Friday.
ii)   . . . by this time next week.
iii)   . . . throughout the whole week.
iv)   . . . for the past week.
v)   . . . before or on Thursday.
vi)   . . . till about Wednesday.
vii)   . . . till after midnight.

2 Look at this timetable and answer the questions that follow it.

Monday to Friday

		London Euston	Coventry	Birmingham International	Birmingham New Street	Wolver-hampton
		dep	arr	arr	arr	arr
	⬛	0650	0823B	0834B	0850B	0916B
×	⬛	0740	0850	0901	0918	0939
×	⬛	0810	0920	0931	0948	1024A
×	⬛	0840	0950	1001	1018	1037
×	⬛	0910	1020	1031	1048	1125A
×	⬛	0935	1045	1057	1114	1134
×	⬛	1005	1123	1133	1151	
×	⬛	1040	1153	1203	1222	1241
×	⬛	1110	1223	1233	1252	1325A
×	⬛	1140	1253	1303	1322	1341
×	⬛	1210	1323	1333	1352	1421A
×	⬛	1240	1353	1403	1422	1441
×	⬛	1310	1423	1433	1452	1523A
×	⬛	1340	1451	1503	1522	1541
×	⬛	1410	1523	1533	1552	
×	⬛	1440	1551	1603	1622	1641
×	⬛	1510	1623	1633	1652	1715
×	⬛	1540	1646	1657	1714	1734
×	⬛	1610	1720	1731	1748	1821A
×	⬛	1640	1746	1757	1814	1833
×	⬛	1710	1818	1828	1846	1905
	⬛	1740	1848	1859	1916	1936
×	⬛	1810	1916	1927	1944	2003
×	⬛	1840	1946	1957	2014	2033
×	⬛	1910	2016	2027	2044	2105
		1940	2051	2102	2119	2143
	⬛	2030	2136	2147	2204	2225
		2140	2250	2301	2321	2341

		Wolver-hampton	Birmingham New Street	Birmingham International	Coventry	London Euston
		dep	dep	dep	dep	arr
×	⬛	0600	0618	0628	0640	0800
×	⬛	0630	0648	0658	0710	0829
×	⬛	0700	0718	0728	0740	0855
×	⬛	0730	0748	0758	0810	0925
×	⬛	0800	0818	0828	0840	0955
×	⬛	0830	0848	0858	0910	1029
×	⬛	0900	0918	0928	0940	1055
×	⬛	0930	0948	0958	1010	1135
×	⬛	0946A	1018	1028	1040	1202
×	⬛	1030	1048	1058	1110	1233
×	⬛	1047A	1118	1128	1140	1302
×	⬛	1130	1148	1158	1210	1333
×	⬛	1142A	1218	1228	1240	1405
×	⬛	1230	1248	1258	1310	1433
×	⬛	1246A	1318	1328	1340	1505
×	⬛	1330	1348	1358	1410	1533
×	⬛	1343A	1418	1428	1440	1605
×	⬛	1430	1448	1458	1510	1633
	⬛	1445A	1518	1528	1540	1702
×	⬛	1530	1548	1558	1610	1736
×	⬛	1546A	1618	1628	1640	1800
×	⬛	1630	1648	1658	1710	1830
		1647A	1718	1728	1740	1858
	⬛	1730	1748	1758	1810	1931
		1745A	1818	1828	1840	2003
		1830	1848	1858	1910	2028
×	⬛	1904	1929	1941	1953	2111
	⬛	1940	2003	2013	2025	2143
		2130	2148	2158	2210	2328

A – Change at Birmingham New Street.   B – Change at Rugby   Valid until 15 May

a) Are these times valid for every day?
b) From when is the timetable itself no longer valid?
c) How quickly can you get from London to Birmingham New Street?
d) What time is the earliest train from Birmingham International to London?
e) What time must you leave London if you want to get to Wolverhampton by 10.30 am, without changing?
f) How long would it take you if you caught the 12.30 train from Wolverhampton to London?
g) If you leave Wolverhampton at 9.30 am and arrive back there at 5.15 pm, how long will you spend in London?

3 Complete this paragraph by using suitable prepositions and information from the timetable.

Stephanie Jamieson is a journalist. Tomorrow she's going to Birmingham to write an article about the Motor Show. The show opens . . . nine o'clock, and to arrive at Birmingham International station . . . that time she must leave London at . . . . Stephanie can only stay at the show . . . one o'clock, as she is meeting a colleague in the centre of Birmingham . . . one-thirty, and the train at . . . will get her to New Street station . . . one twenty-five. . . . the afternoon she will stay at her colleague's office, and then she'll catch the . . . train from Birmingham

New Street to meet a friend in
Wolverhampton at a quarter . . . five.
She wants to be back in London . . .
eight-thirty, so she'll catch the . . . train
back. As she is on the train . . . almost
. . . hours she will be able to write her
article . . . her journey.

4 Look at these two pages from a diary
and then write as much as you can
about this person's week, using the
prepositions you have been practising.

For example: *On Tuesday she's
catching the half past nine train to
Cambridge.*

MON 2	FRI 6
AM - New secretary starts 2·30 - Meeting 6·30 - J + F for drinks	12·30 - Meet Gemma, take to pantomime 7·00 - Return to Frank's for dinner
TUES 3	SAT 7
9·30 - Train to Cambridge 12·30 - Lunch with Cambridge Sales Manager	10·30 - Hairdresser 8·00 - Meet G. at Leicester Sq. Odeon
WED 4	SUN 8
Cambridge	
THURS 5	NOTES
Cambridge 4·45 - Train to London 7·30 - Badminton lesson	Don't forget documents for Liverpool next week

5 Fill in this crossword using the clues
below. Each answer is a preposition.

ACROSS

1 We have to attend school . . . to
the age of 16 in Britain.
4 How can they expect us to do this
exam . . . three hours?
6 Meet me . . . nine o'clock on the dot.
7 They stayed at the hospital . . .
7.30 till midnight.
9 He hasn't been perfectly healthy
. . . his last illness.
10 She lived in Brazil . . . several years.
11 I'll return your book to you . . .
I've read it.

DOWN

2 Surely you're not going out now? It's
. . . eleven o'clock.
3 I'll get to the hospital . . . an hour.
5 I learnt a lot of Russian . . . my stay
in Moscow.
8 It is advisable to book at least three
months . . . departure to ensure a
place on the holiday.

43

SECTION FOUR

WAYS AND MEANS

This section is divided into four categories:

1	Why? Because . . .	*(cause and reason)*
2	What with?	*(instrument and means)*
3	How?	*(manner)*
4	What for?	*(purpose)*

All the prepositions in this section express abstract relationships between actions and their reasons, causes, the manner in which they were done etc.

1   WHY? BECAUSE . . .

because of   due to   for   from   of   out of   owing to through   with

because of   Reason or motive for an action

Every European country has high unemployment at the moment. Most people say it's because of the world recession.

due to   Reason for an action (usually external)

That exam was eventually discontinued, due to the high failure rate

for   Reason for an action, often based on conviction

Freedom fighters are often prepared to die for their beliefs.

from   Cause of an action/state (usually natural)

Thousands of people are suffering from malnutrition in the Third World.

of   Cause of an action (usually internal)

The cause of the accident was brake failure.

out of   Motive, often unconscious, underlying an action.

He donated £100 out of a deep concern for the old people who had lost their homes.

owing to   Reason for an action (as *due to*)
Owing to the previous night's storms, many roads were closed.

through   Cause of an action/state (usually external)
The argument started through a stupid misunderstanding.

with   Feeling resulting in action
The two dogs glared at each other and trembled with anger.

Set phrases
Die of a broken heart
Jump for joy

EXERCISES

1   Fill in the gaps with a suitable preposition.

    a   The girl fainted . . . lack of oxygen.
    b   . . . the financial knowledge of the new director, the company made a huge profit last year.
    c   Many terrorists have died . . . their cause.
    d   The old couple became very ill . . . the neglect of their families.
    e   At the end of his ordeal the hostage cried . . . joy and relief that it was over.
    f   The woman never told the police about her cruel husband . . . fear that her family would find out.
    g   It is said that swans can die . . . a broken heart if their partners die or disappear.
    h   Many people get hay fever in the summer months . . . the pollen in the air.

2   Put these words into the correct order to make sensible sentences.

    a   family/ lives/ he/ his/ for
    b   trembling/ anger/ I/ not/ am/ fear/ with
    c   abroad/ because of/ situation/ went/ the/ he/ unemployment
    d   tongue/ water/ of/ swelled/ from/ his/ lack
    e   paid/ due/ error/ you/ to/ computer/ were/ not

    f   joined/ society/ concern/ handicapped people/ I/ out of/ for/ this

    g   owing to/ interest/ lecture/ cancelled/ has/ the/ lack/ been/ of

    h   the/ started/ through/ misunderstanding/ fight/ a/ regrettable

3   Fill in this chart with ticks (✓) and crosses (✗) according to the circumstances in which the preposition is usually used. The first two rows have been done for you.

EXAMPLES OF VERBS	BECAUSE OF	DUE TO	FOR	FROM	OF	OUT OF	OWING TO	THROUGH	WITH	NOUNS
	✓	✗	✗	✓	✓	✗	✗	✗	✓	hunger
to die	✓	✗	✗	✗	✓	✓	✗	✗	✓	jealousy
to suffer										fear
										lung failure
to cancel										a mistake
to scream										one's country
										a heart attack
to tremble										cigarette smoking
to jump										neglect
										unemployment
										bad weather
										malnutrition

4   Complete the following sentences based on the chart above.

    a . . . from smoking too many cigarettes.
    b . . . through a dreadful mistake.
    c . . . because of her years of unemployment.
    d . . . with a fear of heights.
    e . . . out of jealousy.
    f . . . due to the bad weather.
    g . . . for their country during the last war.
    h . . . of a massive heart attack.

5   Now make ten more sentences of your own based on the chart. Be careful to make the correct combinations of preposition and noun.

2   WHAT WITH?

by   by means of   via   with

by   Instrument (human or object)
He was killed by a terrorist's bullet.

Means
If you visit me in Hong Kong you'll have to come by air.
He only found out our plans by threatening me.

Agent (as in the passive)
The new shopping centre was built by a private company.

Creator
Have you read the new book by Anthony Burgess?

by means of   Means (more formal than *by*)
The union leader was elected by means of a secret ballot.

via   By way of
The best way to get from London to Brussels is via Ostend.

with   Instrument (usually an object, used with a human subject)
The man shot his wife with a revolver.
Cut that bacon with some scissors, not with a knife.

Set phrases
By air, by road, by sea
By car, by bus, by train, by plane etc.

EXERCISES

1   Fill in the gaps with a suitable preposition.

   a   Which way do you have to go if you travel to Australia
     . . . air?

   b   You go . . . Bahrain.

   c   Most of the buildings in this area were designed . . . the
     same architect.

    d   The spy managed to leave the country . . . a stolen passport.

    e   Police believe that the child was murdered . . . a madman . . . a shotgun.

    f   How long does the journey take . . . bus?

    g   The window was broken . . . a heavy object.

    h   They only heard the bad news . . . a phone call from the press.

2   Make sensible sentences with these phrases.

a) This pub is still lit	i) by budgeting very carefully.
b) The government discovered the wishes of the people	ii) by a 12-volt battery.
c) You'll have more freedom if you come	iii) with an axe.
d) We only managed to save enough	iv) via India.
e) The tree was cut down	v) by gas.
f) Most cars are powered	vi) by means of a referendum.
g) The flats had been painted	vii) by car.
h) The best way to China overland is	viii) with bright pink paint.

3   Complete these sentences, using the diagrams as prompts.

    a   Cut the meat . . .

    b   They sailed to Portugal . . .

    c   The quickest way to France is . . .

    d   They heard the news . . .

    e   Remove grease stains . . .

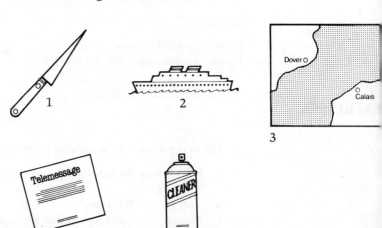

4   Add prepositions and any other necessary words to form full
    sentences from these prompts.

    a   Green/ made/ mixing/ yellow/ blue.
    b   German/ politicians/ elected/ proportional representation.
    c   I/ always/ make/ clothes/ hand.
    d   Parcels/ should/ tied/ string.
    e   Prime Minister/ travelled/ Australia/ Singapore.
    f   All/ dresses/ designed/ Yves St Laurent.
    g   Refugee/ left/ country/ false passport.
    h   You/ can/ go/ road/ air/ to/ Moscow/ not/ sea.

3   HOW?

as   by   like   with

as   In the capacity of someone's profession/habit
         He takes over as managing director next month.

by   By degrees
         'Your son's growing fast, isn't he?' 'Yes, he gets bigger by the day.'

like   Behaviour in the manner of
           He always behaves like a child when he's losing.

with   Have a quality in one's manner
           He conducted the orchestra with spirit and enthusiasm.

Set phrase   *Little by little*

EXERCISES

1   Choose the correct preposition.

    a   The soldier faced the enemy — *by/with/like* — determination.
    b   The film star acted — *as/like/with* — a spoilt child.
    c   You must try to lose weight slowly; just a little week —
        with/as/by — week, or you'll put it on again very quickly.
    d   Politicians who speak — *with/as/like* — sincerity get more
        support from the people.
    e   You should take his advice: he's telling you this — *as/like/
        by* — a solicitor.

2   Put *as* or *like* in the gaps.

   a   I had to work . . . a madman to finish this on time.
   b   He's mentally retarded and he behaves . . . a child when
       he wants something.
   c   Speaking . . . a cook in this prison, I support the
       complaints the health visitor made.
   d   I'm advising you . . . a friend, not . . . a teacher, to give
       your future some serious thought.

3   Paraphrase these sentences, using the preposition given.

   a   The teacher says there isn't much   by
       improvement in her work, but every
       day she's slightly better.
   b   Alcohol makes some people act very foolishly.   like
   c   Watches are made in a very precise way.   with
   d   I don't think I'll be able to convince anyone   with
       that these new plans are good in my report
       as I don't really believe in them myself.
   e   In my medical capacity, I advise you to   as
       get plenty of rest and fresh air.
   f   The apple tree is growing really slowly,   by
       but it's a little bigger each year.

4   WHAT FOR?

for   in   towards

for   Express purpose

Let's not stay here; let's go for a walk.
Those machines are used for making electronic components.

in   Part of a process

Aluminium plate is used in the printing process.

towards   To do something for an express purpose

I'm putting this money towards a good holiday this year.

Set phrase   *Save for a rainy day.*

EXERCISES

1 Choose the correct preposition.

a He'll do anything — *for/in* — money.
b That room is only used — *towards/for* — eating in.
c At the moment I'm putting £10 a week into the bank — *towards/for* — a new car.
d It's going to be an expensive Christmas this year so I'm saving — *for/towards* — it now.
e 'Can I have another five pounds, Mum?'
  'Yes, anything — *towards/for* — a quiet life.'
f 'When is pig-iron used?'
  'It's used — *in/towards* — making steel.'

2 Discuss the purpose of the objects pictured below, using *for* + *-ing*.
  For example: a knife is used for cutting meat.

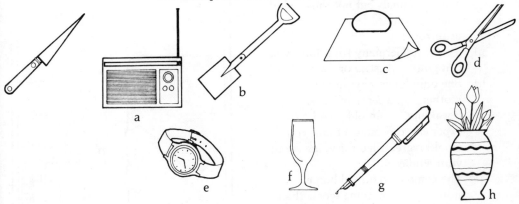

3 The difference between *for* and *in* is that *for* expresses the main purpose of the subject, while *in* suggests that the subject is only one part of the manufacturing process.
Match the subjects with the results, using *for* or *in.*

a) Hops are used	i) the manufacture of glass.
b) Wood-pulp is used	ii) the manufacture of petrol.
c) Sand is used	iii) the generation of electricity.
d) Flour is used	iv) making beer.
e) Lead is used	v) the manufacture of paper.
f) Coal is used	vi) making bread.

CONSOLIDATION OF SECTION FOUR

1   Fill in the gaps with a suitable preposition.

   a)   He was unable to attend the conference . . . illness.

   b)   The prisoners escaped . . . the guard's carelessness.

   c)   We can't afford to eat out at the moment as we're saving . . . a new carpet.

   d)   The kidnapped girl's parents cried . . . relief when they saw their daughter again.

   e)   He's only eighteen but he behaves . . . a man twice his age.

   f)   Capital punishment may deter some criminals but not those who commit crimes . . . a cause, such as terrorists.

   g)   To get to Germany from Italy you can go . . . Austria or Switzerland.

   h)   She only looks after her old mother . . . a sense of duty.

   i)   Speaking . . . an older and more experienced person, I think you would regret it later if you gave up your studies now.

   j)   The climbers returned home, suffering . . . nothing worse than exhaustion.

   k)   The safe had been forced open . . . an iron bar.

   l)   . . . a heavy rainstorm last night, the telephone lines have been out of order today.

   m)   There are very few trains powered . . . steam now.

   n)   If he hadn't threatened me . . . such ferocity, I wouldn't have believed that he was serious.

2   Look at this sketch of a murder, then complete the sentences using the information in the diagram and your imagination.

   a)   The attacker entered the room by . . .
   b)   The attacker killed his victim for . . .
   c)   The victim was killed by . . .
   d)   He killed him with . . .
   e)   The attacker left the room by . . .
   f)   He left the scene of the crime by . . . (transport)

3 Now complete this dialogue between two police officers. Remember to use the prepositions you have been practising.

A What was the motive?
B Well, he wasn't killed for . . .
A No, there was a lot on the table.
B He may have been killed out of . . .
A There's no evidence. He was happily married; some documents have been taken from the safe.
B But the safe was opened with . . .
A Oh, you think the victim opened it?
B Yes, I do. And that's not the only thing he opened. The attacker entered by . . .
A What about the broken window?
B The broken glass was on the outside.
A Oh, so it was broken from the inside. Let me see, Lee was killed with a . . .
B No, with the . . . he was wearing.
A What about the blood?
B His head was cut due to . . .
A Of course. I wonder why he had so much money.
B For . . . He had packed his suitcases.
A He also had an unusual air ticket.
B Yes, it was to the USA . . . Moscow, not direct.
A I think I'm beginning to understand.

4 Fill in this crossword using the clues below. Each answer is a preposition.

ACROSS

1 I'm not buying anything, I'm saving . . . a rainy day.
3 He's improving rapidly, . . . the day.
4 The Orient Express used to run from London to Istanbul . . . Venice.

6 These days tiny microscopes are used . . . delicate surgical operations.
7 The driver ran over the child . . . sheer negligence.
9 Our charity is at present collecting donations . . . a bus to take the children to school.
11 She acts very much . . . a teacher already.
12 The plants all died . . . the same disease.

DOWN

2 . . . his connections, he was not sacked from the company. (5,2)
3 I invited her purely . . . her pleasant husband. (7,2)
5 He spoke . . . much bitterness about the accident.
8 Many students get jobs . . . shop assistants in the summer.
10 She won't leave her sick parents . . . a strong sense of duty. (3,2)

SECTION FIVE

COMPARISON

This section is divided into three categories:

1 Round and about   *(approximation)*
2 Comparing and contrasting   *(comparison and contrast)*
3 Doing sums   *(addition and subtraction)*

All the prepositions in this section express relationships of comparison between two objects, places, people or numbers.

1   ROUND AND ABOUT

about   around   at   by   in   near

about   Approximate position (used without specified noun)
I've looked everywhere but I can't find my magazine. I saw it this morning so it must be somewhere about the place.

Approximate time
Meet me at about midnight.

Here and there
The horses wandered aimlessly all about the field.

around   As *about*, in all three cases
I think he lives somewhere around Athens.
I can only stay around an hour.
Throwing things around the room won't help; try to calm down.

at   Approximate position (not time)
He said he'd meet me at the station but he didn't say exactly where.

by   Approximate, but close, position
They want to move house because they live by the site of the new airport.

in Approximate area, numbers and ages

They're hoping to rent a chalet somewhere in The Alps this year.

near Approximate close position

Don't stand near the fire, you'll burn yourself.

Set phrases *Around and about* *See you around*
In the twenties (i.e. the 1920s)
In his/her twenties (i.e. between the ages of 20 and 29)

EXERCISES

1 Choose the correct preposition.

  a He said he'd meet me immediately after work — *at/near/ about* — his office.

  b The cup-final should finish — *near/in/about* — six-thirty, but it may go on longer if there's extra-time.

  c There are meant to be fish and chip shops all — *near/in/ around* — London, but I haven't seen one.

  d I'd like to visit your colleague who lives — *by/near/at* — Cairo.

  e If we're lucky, we'll be able to spend a few hours — *in/ around/about* — Singapore.

  f The flight will cost — *about/at/near* — a hundred dollars.

  g I'll meet you — *in/by/around* — the ticket office.

  h I don't know her age, but she must be — *in/at/about* — forty.

2 Complete the following sentences.

  a Let's have a picnic by . . .

  b It's a very convenient location, very near . . .

  c If we want to get good seats, we'd better meet about . . .

  d What a badly-matched pair! He's in . . . and she's about . . .

  e He's a shipping millionaire. He owns around . . .

  f Ibiza's great for swimming: there are beautiful beaches all around . . .

3 Make sensible sentences from these phrases.

a) According to the map there are good views of the mountains

b) Did you know that Victor Hugo lived somewhere

c) Don't go too

d) She lives

e) My grandparents love having young people

f) I'd like to spend a week

g) The boat journey takes

h) Wouldn't it be nice to live

i) She looks young but she's

i) near the sea.

ii) at a lakeside resort this year.

iii) around this part of Paris?

iv) about ten hours.

v) in the north of Sweden, but I don't know which town.

vi) about fifty.

vii) around the whole of this area.

viii) in the mountains?

ix) around them.

4 Express the relationships shown in these diagrams. For example:

The bus stop is near the school.

a

b

c

d

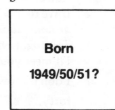

Born 1949/50/51?

e

f

5 How's your geography? Express approximate relationships using these prompts.

a Versailles/Paris

b Colisseum/Rome

c Alps/Switzerland

d Crown Jewels/Tower of London

e Australia/New Zealand

f mines/the north of England

2 COMPARING AND CONTRASTING

after against below beside between like near over
under unlike up to

after
Comparable to
This new artist's work is after the style of Rousseau.

against
Contrasting with
You need to show that picture against a dark background.

Compared with
Look at these figures against last year's; they're so much better this year.

below
Less/fewer than
Shopkeepers are asked to keep their price increases below the rate of inflation.

beside
Compared with
Beside her sister she's not in the least beautiful.

between
Differentiating two things
She's so colour-blind she can't tell the difference between blue and green.

like
Similar to
You've gone so brown, you look like an Italian.

near
Similar to/approaching
No one can come near him in stupidity.

over
More than, a greater number/amount than
He's got over ten thousand stamps in his collection.

under
Less/fewer than
The Ecology Party got under a thousand votes in my area.

unlike
Not similar to
That child is unlike either of its parents.

up to   Compared to normal

This work isn't up to your normal standard; aren't you feeling well?

Set phrases

Up to scratch (the required standard)
Under the weather (ill)

EXERCISES

1 Fill in the gaps with a suitable preposition.

   a Good grief! The child's temperature is . . . 103°F.
   b As you're wearing a dark dress for this photo you'd better stand . . . a light background.
   c You're old enough to know the difference . . . right and wrong.
   d That smells . . . something burning. Are you sure you turned the cooker off?
   e Video recorders are becoming cheaper; you can now get older models for . . . £300.
   f I'm afraid the beauty of the Alps is nothing . . . that of the Dolomites.
   g You need a few more driving lessons. I don't think you're . . . test standard yet.
   h That new German author writes very much . . . the style of Böll.

2 Provide questions for the following answers.

   For example: No, under a hundred pounds a week.
   Question: *Do you earn a lot?*

   a Over 1.50 metres.
   b No, more like my mother, really.
   c Yes, it is, but not beside St. Peter's in Rome.
   d You have to be over eighteen.
   e Not up to the usual standard, no.
   f No, it just looks like leather.
   g In France it's below 10% at the moment.
   h No, she's unlike me in most ways, except that we're both fair.

3 Paraphrase the following sentences using the preposition given.

a You really don't know if that's margarine or butter, do you? — **between**

b You have to be eighteen to vote. You're not old enough. — **under**

c Fourteen! But the cookery class can only take twelve people. — **over**

d The sound of that instrument is very similar to a guitar. — **like**

e An orange background? But won't red clash? — **against**

f You think she's stupid? You should meet her husband. — **near**

g I don't think she's good enough to join my class. — **up to**

4 Look at this information about population levels.

COUNTRY	AREA (KM²)	POPULATION	NUMBER OF PEOPLE PER KM² (DENSITY)
Greenland	2,176,000	56,000	0.02
Hong Kong	1,000	4,514,000	4,320
USSR	22,402,000	262,402,000	12
UK	244,000	55,852,000	229
USA	9,363,000	216,817,000	23
Malta	300	332,000	1,051
Lebanon	10,000	3,056,000	294
China	9,597,000	958,030,000	90
India	3,288,000	625,018,000	190

Now answer these questions.

Which countries in the chart have:
a an area of over 5,000,000 square kilometres?
b an area of under 1,000,000 square kilometres?
c a population of over 100,000,000 people?
d a population of under 1,000,000 people?
e a population density of over 100 people per sq km?
f a population density of under 100 people per sq km?

5   Now look at this paragraph about Malta.

Malta is a small country with just over 300,000 inhabitants. It is under five hundred square kilometres in area, but has a population density of over one thousand people per square kilometre. It is like Hong Kong, in that they both have small land areas, but the difference between them is that Hong Kong's population is much higher.

Write similar paragraphs about Greenland, Hong Kong, Russia and China, and also about your own country, if you know the statistics. (Be careful not to use the above as an exact model as each paragraph will be slightly different.)

3   DOING SUMS

besides   divided by   in addition to   minus   plus   times (together) with

besides   As well as

I've got three other dogs, besides the dachshund.

divided by   (Used only in arithmetic)   *Ten divided by two is five.*

in addition to   As well as, besides

In addition to a 20% pay-rise the workers are asking for a reduction in the number of hours per week.

minus   Without

The explorers returned to base minus their native guide, who had fallen 500 metres to his death.

Subtraction (only arithmetic)

Ten minus six equals four.

plus   As well as

The whole family arrived at once, plus the two dogs.

Addition (only arithmetic)

Three plus four equals seven.

times   Multiplication (only arithmetic)

Three times three equals nine.

(together) with   Working with something

*Her intelligence and enthusiasm, together with her confidence,
make her the ideal candidate.*

EXERCISES

1   Fill in the gaps with a suitable preposition.

   a   This establishment only accepts animals if they have had a
       flu vaccination, . . . an enteritis one.
   b   . . . cuts in defence and education spending, the
       government has cut back on the health service.
   c   Two hundred and three . . . seventy-nine equals two
       hundred and eighty-two.
   d   They took two bottles of wine, some cans of beer, . . . a
       bottle of whisky to the party.
   e   If you look at our income alone, it seems very good, but if
       you look at it . . . all our expenditure, you'll see why
       we're worried.
   f   By your illogical reckoning two . . . two is five.
   g   You can't expect your doctor to devote so much time to
       you; she's very busy, . . . the fact that you're never really
       ill!
   h   £200,000! Pretty good for two hours' work, isn't it? Right,
       . . . four that's £50,000 each, OK?

2   Match these questions to the answers below them.

   a   How do you work out the current of an electrical appliance?
   b   How many rooms does this house have?
   c   Why do you think you failed the exams, Miss Jones?
   d   How do you change fractions into percentages?
   e   Why was there a strike last week?

   i)   The fraction times one hundred.
   ii)   A lot of reasons: new timetables, the sacking of one
         worker, general unrest, plus more money of course.
   iii) Eight, besides the kitchen and bathroom.
   iv)   Well, I was working every evening in a restaurant, in
         addition to the Saturday job at the supermarket.
   v)   The formula is: current equals voltage divided by
         resistance.

CONSOLIDATION OF SECTION FIVE

1 Fill in the gaps with a suitable preposition.

a) Can you really not tell the difference . . . plastic and leather?

b) It's no good saying that the train leaves . . . midnight; you'd better be more precise.

c) The architecture of the new church is rather . . . the style of Wren.

d) Two 'steak and chips' and a bottle of wine? That's fifteen pounds, . . . ten percent service. Sixteen pounds, fifty, please.

e) The lift won't move if there are . . . ten people in it.

f) Three new halls of residence are being built . . . the university campus.

g) If you look at this year's figures for deaths on the road . . . last year's, you'll see that the seat-belt law is effective.

h) There are still many people in this country who live . . . the official poverty level.

i) We bought the house for £5,000 in 1970 and sold it for £19,000 last year. That's almost four . . . the original value.

j) He's invited all his relatives to the wedding . . . about twenty friends.

2 Look at the chart below and provide the questions for these answers.

For example: Only one under ten pounds.

Question: *How many hotels are there in the area for under ten pounds a night? (Or anything similar.)*

a) The differences between a hotel and an inn are the price, facilities and size.

HOTEL	DISTANCE	BEDS	FACILITIES	PRICE (Double Room)	BREAKFAST	MEALS
Sheraton	15 km.	200 – 220	Swimming pool, bar, restaurant	from £56.00	included	in Restaurant from £8.00
Kings	2 km.	75 – 80	bar, restaurant	£44.00	included	in restaurant from £10.00
Crosstown Motel	5 km.	approx 70	games room, bar, restaurant	£42.50	£2.50	in restaurant from £5.00
Bear Hotel	4 km.	approx 30	bar, restaurant	£26.30	included	set menu £10.00
Red Lion Inn	8 km	16	bar	£18.22	included	bar snacks
Old Village Inn	next door	18		£16.20	£2.00	
Smith's family Hotel	2 km	10	bar	£14.16	included	£5.00
Ethel's Guest House	½ km.	4		£ 9.00	included	3.00

b) Two are very near here.
c) It's five kilometres from here, by the motorway.
d) Only two actually in the village.
e) I'm afraid it doesn't come anywhere near the others in quality.
f) It has about seventy beds.
g) No, only one has over two hundred beds.
h) It's not up to hotel standard, but it's better than the usual guest house.

3 Compare the hotels, using the prepositions you have been practising, like this:

The Sheraton isn't near the village. It's got over two hundred beds and its price is higher than the prices of the other hotels. It has good facilities: a swimming pool and a restaurant, in addition to the usual bar.

Breakfast is included in the price but other meals have to be taken in the restaurant and usually cost over ten pounds. Therefore, bed and breakfast, plus evening meal for two, wouldn't come to under seventy pounds. Beside the other hotels around the area it's good but rather expensive.

4 Complete this conversation in the tourist office, referring to the chart in Exercise 2.

Official: Can I help you?
Customer: Yes, I'd like to book a double room in a hotel near . . .
Off: Certainly, there are two hotels very near here, but several others . . .

Cus: That's OK, I've got a car.
Off: What kind of hotel would you like?
Cus: Quite a small one, with a bar.
Off: Well, the Bear Hotel has about . . .
Cus: That's OK. Can we get an evening meal there?
Off: It has a restaurant, with set meals at . . .
Cus: Mmm, about how much do the rooms cost?
Off: About . . .
Cus: So for the room plus . . . that would be over . . .
Off: That's right, it certainly wouldn't be under . . .
Cus: Mmm, do you have anything else, under . . .?
Off: Well, there's Smith's Family Hotel. That's very near . . .
Cus: How much would that be?
Off: Around . . .
Cus: And for a meal?
Off: About five pounds each so you'd pay . . .
Cus: That's about twenty-four pounds, so for four nights I'd pay?
Off: Twenty-four . . . four, that's ninety-six pounds.
Cus: That would be fine. Will you book it for me please?

5 Write a similar dialogue to the above between the tourist officer and

a) a family of six looking for the cheapest hotel possible;
b) a businessman who wants to leave early, without breakfast;
c) a group of tourists.

6 Fill in this crossword using the clues below. Each answer is a preposition.

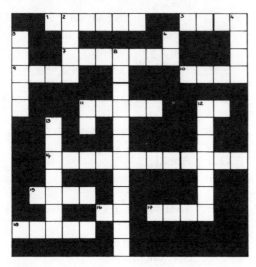

ACROSS

1 Although they're twins, they're quite . . . each other.

3 Most children look . . . their parents in some way. (2,2)

7 Look at these slides . . . a very light background.

9 The zoo has . . . 200 types of animal.

10 He won the elections with a huge majority. None of the other candidates came anywhere . . . him.

11 I'm sorry, Sir. We can't let you in because you're . . . eighteen.

12 You can't miss the car park; it's . . . the station.

14 You need all these . . . a power supply to operate the computer. (8,4)

15 Don't put those papers . . . the window; they'll blow away.

16 She's only . . . her twenties, very young to have such a responsible job.

17 Ten . . . ten equals twenty.

18 Fifteen . . . five equals ten.

DOWN

2 If the soup gets . . . boiling point, the cream will separate.

4 If your temperature goes . . . 100°F, call the doctor.

5 We can catch the six o'clock bus, it's . . . ten to now.

6 You'll find him . . . the college at this time of day.

8 . . . his problems at work, he's got very bad problems with his teenage children. (2,8,2)

11 Your work isn't . . . to scratch; are you feeling well?

12 . . . the language problems, people also have problems living abroad because of the cultural differences.

13 The difference . . . you and me is that I'm diplomatic and you're completely tactless!

SECTION SIX

GROUP RELATIONSHIPS

This section is divided into five categories:

1 For and against   *(support and opposition)*
2 In and out   *(inclusion and exclusion)*
3 All of these but . . .   *(exception)*
4 What about?   *(relating to, concerning)*
5 Staying or leaving   *(attachment and separation)*

All the prepositions in this section express the relationship of one object or person to another.

---

1 FOR AND AGAINST

against   behind   contrary to   for   for the sake of
in favour of   in support of   opposite   with

against To be contrary to something
Why are you against everything our society believes in?

Not to give support to
The Labour Party is against Britain remaining in the EEC.

behind Give support to idealogically
Are you behind the nurses' strike?

Give financial support to, provide ideas for
The Swiss government was behind the building of some of the Alpine passes.

contrary to The opposite of
Strangely, all his ideas are contrary to those of the working classes.

for To favour doing something (usually when with a group of people)
Well, I'm for turning back. It's too dangerous to go mountain climbing in this weather.

For someone's benefit
Come on, wash your face for Daddy.

for the sake of For someone's benefit
Can't you be quiet for once, if not for me then for the baby's sake

in favour of Be in agreement
Are you in favour of capital punishment?

in support of For the benefit of
I'm trying to raise money in support of the Campaign for Nuclear Defence.

opposite (to) Not be in agreement
His ideas are completely opposite to mine.

with Be in agreement (with a person or idea)
It's a very good plan. I'm with you all the way.

Set phrases
Contrary to popular belief/opinion
For Pete's sake! (expresses exasperation)

EXERCISES

1 Fill in the gaps with a suitable preposition.

a The Conservative government are . . . building as many new private homes as possible.

b Many incompatible couples stay together . . . their children

c . . . popular opinion, the only way to lose weight is to eat less.

d A lot of people know that tax evasion is . . . the law but do not consider it a crime.

e We just can't agree. Her opinions on this subject are totally . . . mine.

f Many policemen and women are . . . capital punishment because they think it would make their jobs easier.

g He won't do anything . . . me while I'm ill.

h The local council is . . . our plans to build new sports facilities in this town.

2 Match each statement with a response below. The response always states the opposite.

a I'm voting in favour of the Ecology Party.
b I think his ideas are contrary to public welfare.
c I'm with Geoff's group on this point.
d We'd better go to the party, for Jenny's sake.
e I'm really against cuts in education.

Responses

i) Oh really? I'm for cuts there rather than in health.
ii) I'm totally against that party.
iii) Sorry! I'm against what Geoff says.
iv) I think he really works for the sake of public welfare.
v) I'm against going for anyone's sake. We should go because we want to.

3 Put these words in the correct order to make sensible sentences.

a International Monetary Fund/ plan/ government's/ the/ behind/ is/ the/ revive/ to/ steel industry/ the
b as soon as/ party/ for/ I'm/ a/ possible/ having
c his ideas/ football team/ behind/ are/ the/ new
d you/ in favour of/ are/ liberation/ women's?
e there's/ law/ driving/ a/ against/ drinking/ and

4 Paraphrase these sentences, using the preposition given.

a All his beliefs are opposed to mine. **contrary to**
b I agree wholeheartedly with your plans **for**
to restructure the company.
c I'm not in favour of siting Cruise **against**
missiles in Europe.
d Do you agree with his plans for a secret **in favour of**
ballot?
e My brother's business is really being **behind**
supported by my father.

5 Using the prepositions you have been practising, express your ideas on the following subjects.

Capital punishment   Violence on TV   Bloodsports
Working mothers   Abortion   Lowering the voting age

2 IN AND OUT

among around beside between beyond in inside of
out of outside round under within without

among
In a group
Your ten-year-old brother is the only sensible one among us.

In the number of
The 1812 Overture is reckoned among Tchaikowsky's best works.

around
Surrounding, on every side of
Sharks were swimming around the tiny boat.

Encircling, enclosing
The wall around the castle was two metres thick.

beside
Not related to (in certain set phrases)
That question is beside the point; we're talking about today, not last year.

between
Flanked by two people, objects, points etc.
Please take a seat between the two men in the corner.

beyond
At a further point
He doesn't live in the village, he lives beyond those fields.

Outside the range of
That car really is beyond repair. Why don't you get a new one?

in
Defined within certain limits
They'll never find him in this crowded room.

inside
Defined within certain limits (three-dimensional)
All the sale items are inside that box.

of
Included among
One of the best films I've ever seen is 'Gone with the Wind'.

out of
Outside the range of
The space shuttle is now out of sight.

outside Beyond the limits of

I'm afraid there's nothing the court can do; it's outside our jurisdiction.

round Encircling, enclosing (as *around*)

It's as though he's built a wall round himself to keep everyone out.

under In the field of

Look for the word under Linguistics if it isn't filed under Speech.

within Not further than, in the limits of

In the Middle Ages people always lived within the walls of their town.
The house is within five minutes' walk of the underground station.

without excluding

It is important that all officers attend the meeting without exception.

Set phrases

Beside the point/question
Between you and me
Beyond help/despair/relief/comprehension
Out of range/sight/luck/reach
Out of sight, out of mind

EXERCISES

1 Change this sentence according to the prompts.

For example: *They found the hidden treasure outside the castle grounds.*
Prompt: the hills over there
They found the hidden treasure beyond the hills over there.

a	the trees	e	the state boundaries
b	the two large stones	f	the city walls
c	the old dining-room	g	the church and the town hall
d	a small jewellery-box	h	the paintings in the art gallery

2 Fill in the gaps with a suitable preposition.

a Your villa is . . . a wonderful position.
b You'll find Renoir listed . . . Impressionists.
c I'd like all . . . the directors to attend the meeting.
d He's totally unfit and . . . condition.
e She's lived . . . the Zulus in South Africa.
f An electrified fence . . . the house will put off burglars.
g People sometimes try to live . . . society by buying small farms, growing all their own food and trying to be self-sufficient.
h Our new classification scheme lists books . . . their title, not the subject.
i This is extremely urgent. We must leave for London . . . delay.

3 Express the relationship of the buildings to the landscape in these diagrams.

For example:

The castle is beyond the stream.

a

b

c

d

e

4 Paraphrase these sentences, using the prepositions given.

a There was one policeman on my left, another on my right.   **between**
b You don't think about me when I'm not here.   **out of**

70

c	Those two seem to be protected by an invisible wall; nothing ever touches them.	**around**
d	I think 'The Tempest' is possibly Shakespeare's best play.	**among**
e	Some people always live within the limitations of their own experience.	**outside**
f	I'm sorry, but I don't think there's any hope for your brother now.	**beyond**
g	If you want to find their phone number, try *his* name, not hers.	**under**
h	The person we're looking for has not left this house.	**inside**

5 Complete these phrases with the correct prepositions to form accepted phrases in English. (Use a dictionary if necessary.)

Preposition	Phrase
Out of	sight
_____	mind
_____	the question
_____	his great works
_____	doubt
_____	you and me
_____	belief
_____	the point
_____	luck
_____	one's experience

---

3 IF NOT FOR . . .

apart from   barring   but   but for   except/except for/excepting

apart from With the exception of

I like all competitive sports apart from rugby.

barring Unless something unexpected happens

Barring an accident the winner of the 1985 French Grand Prix will be the current leader, Kaufmann.

but   With the exception of

Everyone but John passed the exam.

but for   If it were not for

But for the unreliable climate, Britain could attract far more tourists.

except   Not including, other than (used to refer back to the subject or object of a main clause)

Everything was wonderful except the food.

except for   As *except*, but used more generally

It was a wonderful holiday except for the food.

excepting   As *except*, slightly more formal

N.B.   *Apart from, except, except for* and *excepting* are usually interchangeable.

EXERCISES

1   Fill in the gaps with a suitable preposition.

   a   I've finished all my exams, . . . French literature.
   b   All those who were invited came, . . . the mayor of the town.
   c   I like eating all types of poultry . . . duck.
   d   . . . bad weather, we'll enjoy ourselves.
   e   I'm interested in all sports, . . . those that are very violent.
   f   She's taking everything . . . the kitchen sink.

2   Make sensible sentences from these phrases.

a)	They were all former champions	i) except South Africa.
b)	The motorway was almost deserted	ii) apart from fishing.
c)	The match between Lendl and McEnroe will start at 2.00	iii) except for the occasional lorry.
d)	He despises all women	iv) apart from the men's finalist.
e)	All the countries competed	v) but his mother.
f)	I disagree with most forms of hunting	vi) barring rain.

3 Find the odd one out in each of these groups and express it in the following way.

For example: tea/ coffee/ coca-cola/ cocoa
They are all hot drinks apart from coca-cola.

a whisky/ brandy/ coca-cola/ sherry
b crimson/ scarlet/ rose/ turquoise
c Lendl/ Becker/ McEnroe/ Maradona
d Spain/ Italy/ Germany/ India
e London/ Paris/ Bonn/ New York

4 WHAT ABOUT?

about   after   as for   as to   at   for   in   of   on   over

about Concerning a particular subject
Why on earth are you talking about farming?

after Show concern about someone
Did you think to ask after Aunt Margaret's health?

as for With regard to (often derogatory)
. . . and as for your ridiculous ideas, I don't want to hear any more.

as to Concerning (more formal than *as for*)
As to the question of finance, the bank has agreed to make a loan of ten thousand.

With regard to (often derogatory like *as for*)
As to the latest offer, the union will write a reply, expressing disgust.

at Regarding a particular subject area
She's very good at English, but not at foreign languages.

for Representing
He's the Member of Parliament for Liverpool East.

in As at (not used with *good* or *bad*)
I'm interested in the sciences, but I'm weak in mathematics.

73

of The subject of a story/ book/ lecture etc.

The subject of today's lecture is 19th century social problems.
He's written a book of poems.

on As *about*, but looking at the general, not the specific

It's a film on the Crimean War, but particularly about Florence Nightingale.

over To express feeling concerning something

She's crying over her broken love affair.

EXERCISES

1 Choose the correct preposition.

    a He's been earning a lot of money since he started working — *for/in/of* — Ferranti.

    b I didn't think anyone could cry so much — *over/about/ for* — such a sentimental film.

    c If you feel sorry — *at/in/for* — handicapped people, why don't you offer to do some voluntary work to help them?

    d He's written a very good thesis — *on/over/as to* — mechanical engineering.

    e I can't stand Beverley, and — *as for/about/for* — her sister, well!

    f It was very nice of your friend to ask — *at/on/after* — me; she hardly knows me.

2 Make sensible sentences from these phrases.

a) She's extremely good	i) in Business Studies.
b) Tomorrow's lecture is	ii) for the Labour Party.
c) I've got lots of books	iii) on the evolution of dinosaurs.
d) Eddy's out canvassing	iv) over a medieval tragedy?
e) He's written a book	v) after your father. How is he?
f) How can you cry so much	vi) at cooking exotic dishes.
g) I forgot to ask	vii) of poetry.
h) My brother's got a degree	viii) about butterflies.

3 In each of the following sentences two of the given alternatives are acceptable, the other is not. Which one is incorrect in each case?

a I work for — *myself/a company/a good film.*
b He's speaking in — *Polish/oriental philosophers/the debate.*
c I know quite a lot about — *physics/your health/people.*
d I can't help crying over — *good books/sad films/exams.*
e Kevin's quite good at — *making friends/your friends/ public speaking.*
f She's written several articles on — *a journal/fishing/cooking.*

5 STAYING OR LEAVING

apart from   away from   behind   from   of   off   on   out of
past   to   with   without

apart from   At a distance, not close to
They're so attached that they can't bear to be apart from each other, not even for a day.

away from   At a distance (physically)
She moved away from London when she left home at eighteen.

behind   No longer with one (usually refers to bad periods in one's life)
I'm glad my student days are behind me now. I couldn't bear to have to do any more exams.

from   Point of origin
She comes from Indonesia.
I learnt that from my mother.

Detachment of something
The robbers took all the money from the bank.

of   Possession
The houses of Southern Spain are usually white-washed.

75

Point of separation, departure

Young animals soon become independent of their mothers.
The winner of the cat show is of Persian parentage.

off Detachment or separation (two dimensional)

Keep off the grass.
The branch fell off the tree when the child sat on it.

on Attachment (two dimensional)

I've never been on a horse in my life!

out of Detachment (three dimensional)

I'm glad I'm out of that awful class at last!

to Attachment of one thing to another

That book belongs to me.
As a child she was very attached to her uncle.

with Attachment

Both my grandparents still live with my parents.

without Separated

No-one can live without friends.

EXERCISES

1 Think about the prepositions above. Which ones refer to attachment in some way, and which refer to detachment? Do any refer to both? Fill in this chart, using the examples to help you.

	APART FROM	AWAY FROM	BEHIND	FROM	OF	OFF	ON	OUT	TO	WITH	WITHOUT
ATTACHMENT											
SEPARATION											
BOTH											

2 Change this sentence according to the prompts.
For example: *Marianne spends a lot of time <u>with</u> her cousins.*
Prompt: her family

   *Marianne spends a lot of time apart from her
   family.*

   a   her bicycle   d   any friends
   b   the safety of her home   e   her home
   c   her boyfriend   f   a boat on the canal.

3 Fill in the gaps with a suitable preposition.

   a   Don't worry about my history of depression; it's . . . me
       now.
   b   You've told me so much about your brother that I feel
       very close . . . him, although I haven't met him yet.
   c   I'm afraid you're not allowed to sit . . . that lawn.
   d   That quotation comes from the last page . . . the book.
   e   The horse is a real thoroughbred; he's . . . purely Arabian
       stock.
   f   Columbus didn't actually come . . . Spain, he just sailed
       . . . there.
   g   Tasmania is an island just . . . the coast . . . South
       Australia.
   h   Yes, he was in prison for two years, but that's all . . . him
       now.

4 Put these words into the correct order to form questions.
   (Note that prepositions often come at the end of questions.)

   a   country/ Karl Marx/ from/ which/ come/ did?
   b   take/ with/ sugar/ tea/ you/ without/ or/ do?
   c   far/ the USA/ from/ is/ how/ the USSR/ away?
   d   animals/ which/ on/ find/ a/ do/ mane/ you?
   e   does/ Japan/ flag/ have/ moon/ the/ national/ on/ of/ a/
       it?
   f   India/ is/ coast/ of/ island/ off/ the/ which/ southern?

5 Now answer the questions above with full sentences, using a
   preposition in each case. (Find out any answers that you don't
   know.)

CONSOLIDATION OF SECTION SIX

1 Read this review of a film. Fill in the gaps with a suitable preposition.

Review of Richard Attenborough's 'Gandhi'.

. . . doubt one . . . the greatest films this decade, 'Gandhi' follows the story . . . Mohandas (Mahatma) Gandhi . . . his days as a young lawyer in South Africa . . . his death. Gandhi found the racial prejudice in South Africa shocking, but the situation in his country horrified him even more, particularly the hostility . . . Muslim and Hindu. He was . . . prejudice of any kind and was never . . . violent action by anybody to achieve their aims. Torn . . . his conscience and the law, he tried to teach his fellow men to face the injustices, not to run . . . them, and to fight peacefully . . . their country's independence. He worked . . . his people and he tried to introduce a life . . . fear, poverty and hatred into his country. . . . popular opinion, Gandhi was not a weak, religious guru, but he was . . . doubt one of the greatest men this century.
The acting throughout is superb, especially as all the parts, . . . a few main characters, were played by Indians. . . . the quality of the filming, it can certainly be counted . . . the best examples of films classified . . . cinematic art.

2 Complete these sentences about the review.

a) This is a review of . . .
b) The film is about . . .
c) It follows the story of . . .
d) Gandhi tried to teach his countrymen to live without . . .
e) Gandhi was against . . .
f) He worked for . . .
g) There was conflict in India between . . .
h) Gandhi led a life of . . .

3 Match each preposition with its opposite from this list.

inside	for
from	outside
within	against
against	to
off	without
in favour of	on

4 Make one sentence using each pair of prepositions above to show the difference between them.

For example: I know most people are in favour of traditional medicine, but I'm against it.

5 In each of the sentences below, change the preposition in the sentence for a similar one, so that the meaning of the sentence does not change.

For example: I like all animals _except_ snakes.

could be: _I like all animals apart from snakes._

a) People who vote for a particular government should then be behind that government in everything it does.

b) Most television detective series are rubbish, and as for the American ones, they're all the same.

c) The examination syllabus for students should be beyond the powers of individual schools.

d) Dogs should be kept off the grass in public parks.

e) Except for the overcooked steak we enjoyed the meal very much.

6 Fill in this crossword using the clues below. Each answer is a preposition.

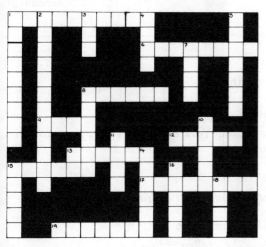

ACROSS

1 The new government is . . . increasing our nuclear defence. (2,6,2)

6 The two parties' views are not totally . . . to each other.

8 The cost of the article is . . . the point; we're discussing the quality.

9 He has already run . . . from the Children's Home several times.

12 I don't believe in ghosts, and . . . people from other planets, it's rubbish! (2,3)

13 Stay . . . the house and keep warm. Then your temperature will go down.

15 It's a very pleasant cottage with trees all . . . it.

17 His views on most things are often, completely . . . to mine, but we still enjoy each other's company.

19 It must be more difficult to live . . . sight than any other sense.

DOWN

1 Nick is doing a lot of campaigning . . . of animal welfare at the moment. (2,7)

2 She's so mean. She'll walk two or three miles rather than take the bus: all . . . thirty pence. (3, 3, 4, 2)

3 You're . . . of luck, there's no milk left.

4 Don't take any sweets . . . strangers.

5 I'm afraid you live . . . our area of responsibility, so we can't help you.

7 She's upset . . . some bad news she had earlier.

8 The stories your young son tells are really . . . belief; they're not true, are they?

10 Ask . . . Mr Creighton's wife while you're there, she's been very ill.

11 Do you take coffee black or . . . milk?

13 I read about it . . . the local newspaper.

14 All the guests are already here . . . one.

15 I've got my tax form somewhere . . . all my documents.

16 The atlases are probably classified . . . geography.

18 At work he's very organised, but . . . his home, it's a mess. (2,2)

SECTION SEVEN

OTHERS

This section deals with categories of prepositions which stand alone, and don't fit into any of the other sections.

1 Is it the right one?   *(circumstance and appropriateness)*
2 Against all odds   *(concession)*
3 What's it made of?   *(material)*
4 Changing round   *(exchange)*

---

1 IS IT THE RIGHT ONE?

by   for   in   under   with

by   In external circumstances

Make sure you arrive in New York by day; it's very dangerous to walk around there by night.

for   Appropriate/suitable

Prince Charles has written books for children.

in   Temporary (personal) circumstances

She's not eating because she's fallen in love.
Don't bother the manager now, he's in a bad mood.

under   According to certain conditions (often set phrases)

The cheque was sent under separate cover.
Under no circumstances will he reconsider his decision.

with   External circumstances decided by a person

I like to sleep with the window open.

Set phrases

By starlight, moonlight etc.   *In a mess*
In good/bad weather etc.   *Under the weather* (unwell)
In his wisdom, stupidity, haste

EXERCISES

1 Choose the correct preposition.

   a Tennis can only be played — *in/by/with* — good weather.
   b How can people sit in smoky rooms — *with/for/in* — all the windows closed?
   c That shop sells magazines marked — *'by/for/with* — adults only'.
   d No-one can be expected to work — *with/under/by* — such awful conditions.
   e Everything looks much more romantic — *by/in/with* — moonlight.
   f It's far too hot in here — *under/for/with* — the central heating on.
   g The crime was committed — *by/under/with* — rather strange circumstances.
   h These sweets are intended — *in/for/by* — diabetics.

2 Make sensible sentences from these phrases.

a) He can't bear blonde women
b) The council has built some flats
c) Venice can seem very sinister
d) The woman had been
e) Don't go riding on the moors
f) I can't concentrate at all
g) Don't ask the boss for a rise today because he's
h) Judges have now turned to community work

i) in foggy weather.
ii) with the television on.
iii) for young criminals.
iv) with very deep tans.
v) in a bad mood.
vi) under a lot of stress.
vii) by night.
viii) for old people.

3 Which prepositions complete these phrases? Use a dictionary if necessary.

   a . . . starlight
   b head over heels . . . love
   c . . . no circumstances
   d books . . . young children
   e . . . good weather
   f not fit . . . young eyes
   g . . . the rush to escape
   h . . . a beard and a moustache

4   Now make eight sentences of your own using the phrases you have completed in Exercise 3.

5   Paraphrase these sentences using the preposition given.

a	This town can be dangerous between ten pm and six am	**by**
b	We need mosquito nets to sleep here.	**with**
c	The document was sent separately.	**under**
d	He's so careless that he lost his passport.	**in**
e	Only disabled people can use this taxi service.	**for**
f	He got out of bed the wrong side this morning.	**in**
g	You'll need the choke out to start the car.	**with**
h	Soft lighting usually makes people look younger.	**by**

2   AGAINST ALL ODDS

despite   for all   in spite of

despite   Disregarding certain conditions (followed by gerund or noun)

Despite the inclusion of the unacceptable clause, the contract was signed.

Despite winning less than 50% of the votes, he became Prime Minister.

for all   As *despite* (usually starts a sentence), suggests effort in vain on the part of the subject

For all her fine clothes, everyone knows how poor she is.

in spite of   As *despite* but less formal (usually followed by noun)

The football match continued, in spite of the awful weather.

EXERCISES

1   Fill in the gaps with a suitable preposition.

   a   . . . her confidence at work, she gets very nervous when she meets new people socially.
   b   We still don't really understand the human brain, . . . our scientific advances.
   c   My house plants always die, . . . the attention and care I give them.
   d   . . . the money he's made, he's not really happy.
   e   . . . the chronic illness she's suffering from, she's always cheerful.
   f   Most of the countries competed in the Olympic Games, . . . their political differences.

2   Change these sentences to use *despite*, *for all* or *in spite of*, but the meaning must remain the same.

   For example: The film was a success, although the critics had given it bad reviews.

   In spite of the bad reviews, the film was a success.
   Despite receiving bad reviews, the film was a success.

   a   Although he's very kind there's something in his manner I don't like.
   b   The tennis match continued, even though it was raining heavily.
   c   He went on gambling, although he'd lost most of his money.
   d   He continued riding horses even after his wife was killed in a fall.
   e   The first space shuttle was not very successful. Nevertheless, the second one was launched soon after.
   f   The government changed in the election. However, the country's problems didn't lessen.

3 WHAT'S IT MADE OF?

from   in   of   out of   with

from   Specific material, not necessarily the main material
I made this bed cover from bits and pieces of material.

in   Material of the instrument used for something, as in works of art
All his sketches are in pencil.

of   Real substance of something (describes the finished product)
Houses are usually made of bricks and mortar.

Substance of character (idiomatic)
Lech Walesa became known as the 'man of iron'.
He's so cruel; he must have a heart of stone.

out of   Specific, often unusual material
The dress was made out of the finest silk.

with   Material inside/added to something (often describes the process of making)
The buns are left to cool and then filled with cream and covered with hot chocolate sauce.

Set phrase
Heart of gold

EXERCISES

1 Fill in the gaps with a suitable preposition.

    a   They're not real flowers; they're made . . . silk.
    b   The loft is insulated . . . fibre glass.
    c   Pillows always used to be filled . . . feathers.
    d   This sculptor always sculpted . . . clay, not stone.
    e   The vase is quite unusual; it's made . . . jade.
    f   A lot of builders today make houses . . . wood again.
    g   This cocktail is made . . . gin, Cointreau, lemon and soda.
    h   Very few pieces of cheap furniture are made . . .real wood, most are made . . . chipboard or plastic.

2   Match these questions with the answers below. Write your answers in full.

   a   What's your wedding ring made of?
   b   What's the cake filled with?
   c   What's your hat made out of?
   d   What's the toothbrush made of?
   e   What was that painting done in?

   bristle and plastic   cream   felt   watercolours   platinum

3   Test your general knowledge by completing these sentences.

   a   The Taj Mahal is made . . .
   b   Leonardo da Vinci usually painted . . .
   c   An omelette is made . . .
   d   Most houses are built . . .
   e   Most windows are made . . .
   f   Pencils are filled . . .
   g   Mayonnaise is made . . .
   h   Someone very kind is described as having a heart . . .

4   Look at this recipe for a chocolate cream cake and fill in the gaps with suitable prepositions.

   1   **To make the cake**: make a paste . . . the butter and sugar. Mix this . . . the eggs and beat vigorously; then fold in the cocoa and flour. Line two baking-tins (made . . . a non-stick material) . . . greaseproof paper and bake for 45 minutes.

   2   **To make the filling**: put the fruit in a saucepan with the kirsch (liqueur made . . . cherries) and bring to the boil. Cover the gelatine . . . a few drops of fruit juice and mix . . . the fruit when spongy. Leave to set.

   3   **To assemble the cake**: split each cake in two, spread one half cake . . . a third of the vanilla cream (made . . . the cream whipped . . . the sugar and vanilla essence) and then spread on a third of the fruit mixture. Repeat with two more cake halves. Cover the whole cake . . . cream and decorate the top . . . grated chocolate.

5   Now look at these ingredients for a recipe and use the model in Exercise 4 and the prompts below to write full instructions. (The first one has been done for you.)

5

TUNA IN PASTRY WITH MUSHROOM SAUCE

Pastry	Tuna mixture	Mushroom sauce
200gm plain flour	1 onion	100gm mushroom
100gm butter	1 can of tuna	25gm butter
pinch of salt	100gm mushrooms	25gm plain flour
water	1 hard-boiled egg	25cl milk
	tomato puree	
	salt and pepper	

---

1   To make the pastry:

Rub/butter/into/flour/salt. Mix/little water. Make/into/soft dough.

Rub the butter into the flour and salt. Mix it with a little water and then make this into a soft dough.

2   To make the tuna mixture:
Fry/onion/mushrooms/mix/tuna.
Make/filling/all/ingredients.

3   To assemble:
Roll/pastry/20 × 20 cm. Line/baking-tray/greaseproof paper. Put/pastry/baking-tray/spread/tuna mixture/then roll up. Bake/45 minutes/hot oven.

4   To make mushroom sauce:
Fry/mushrooms/butter. Make/paste/flour/mushrooms/butter. Slowly stir/milk/boil.

---

4   ALL CHANGE

against   for   from   into   to

against   Give something as a security

Some football clubs take out insurance policies against their star players receiving serious injuries.

for   Exchange of one object in return for another
I'd like to change this coat for a larger size.

Barter of some description
He's getting fifty pounds for five hours' work.

from   Transformation out of a state
From being a pacifist, he changed his ideas completely and joined the army.

Used with *to* or *into*
When he drinks a lot he changes from being a kind, considerate man into a violent hooligan.

into   Transformation (to a new state)
In all fairy stories the frog changes into a handsome prince.

Changing clothes
When I get home from work I change into a T-shirt and jeans. I hate wearing a suit!

to   Transformation (less personal than *into*, can be a habit that is changed)
I'm going to change to a healthier margarine.

EXERCISES

1   Change this sentence according to the prompts.

    For example: Tony was a conservative when he was young.
    Prompt: conservative-socialist
              He changed from being a conservative to a socialist.

    a   monster when he was angry
    b   his family car/smaller one
    c   took a life insurance policy/his mortgage
    d   clean clothes for the evening
    e   better way of living
    f   boy/man
    g   washing machine/better one
    h   shares/cash

2 Fill in the gaps with a suitable preposition.

a If all men could change . . . women for just one day
   there'd be greater understanding between the sexes.
b Nurses get an extremely low salary . . . the long hours
   they work and all their dedication.
c I left my gold watch as security . . . the money I owed the
   shopkeeper.
d When we started the high-fibre diet we changed . . . white
   flour, bread and sugar . . . all wholemeal products.
e It's impossible to take out an insurance policy . . . acts of
   God, such as earthquakes.
f But Mum, Jenny gave me three beetles . . . my pet mouse!
g I'd like to change £100 sterling . . . Japanese Yen, please.
h When he'd spent a year in Poland his ideals changed . . .
   Communism . . . Capitalism.

3 Choose which preposition(s) each of the following diagrams
   expresses best.

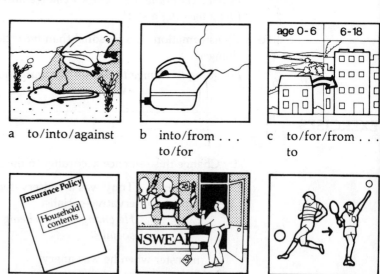

a to/into/against

b into/from . . .
   to/for

c to/for/from . . .
   to

d to/into/against

e from/for/into

f for/from/to

4 Now make sentences to express the ideas in the diagrams
   above.

CONSOLIDATION OF SECTION SEVEN

1 Fill in the gaps with a suitable preposition.
a) Fill the gearbox . . . oil.
b) This wine is intended . . . drinking with the dessert.
c) . . . the heat, all the men had to wear a shirt and tie.
d) I'm just beginning to paint . . . oils.
e) If you whip the cream for long enough it will turn . . . butter.
f) The document will be released only . . . these very strict conditions.
g) 'Would you give up your country cottage . . . a town flat?'
h) 'Not . . . all the tea in China!'
i) . . . his grand speeches he doesn't really understand the basics of the subject.
j) The sauce is made . . . cheese and eggs.

2 Match the questions to the answers below.
a) What is beer made from?
b) How does she keep her flat so warm?
c) Why is she looking so happy?
d) What happened when he stopped smoking?
e) What are your plates made of?
f) When is the best time to see the river illuminations?

Answers
i) Pure Staffordshire pottery.
ii) He turned to drink.
iii) Hops and water.
iv) By moonlight.
v) She's in love.
vi) With an open fire.

3 Paraphrase these sentences using the preposition given.

a **in spite of**
Fabian continued drinking, even though the doctor had told him to stop.

b **against**
Could you lend me £30? I'll give you this watch as security.

c **from . . . to**
Ronald Reagan was an actor, but now he's the President of the USA.

d **from**
We use only the finest ingredients in our cakes.

e **in**
This situation is very difficult for me.

f **into**
After only a couple of months the puppy had become a fully-grown dog.

g **for**
Children are best suited to this kind of comedy.

h **despite**
Although the winter was very cold the rose bush bloomed the next summer.

i **of**
The only material in this jumper is pure new wool.

j **for**
This dress is a bit too small for me. I'm going to take it back to the shop and change it.

4 Which preposition completes each of these phrases?

 a) . . . no circumstances
 b) . . . fresh cream
 c) . . . his stupidity
 d) . . . the radio on
 e) . . . gaslight
 f) . . . pure silk
 g) . . . men only
 h) . . . separate cover

5 Now make sentences from the expressions above.

6 Fill in this crossword, using the clues opposite. Each answer is a preposition.

ACROSS

4 Take advantage of her now, while she's . . . a good mood.
5 . . . the bad lighting, I manage to read under the bedclothes.
6 Two pounds . . . a glass of wine. That's ridiculous!
7 I want to change . . . a different sports centre; one that's cheaper.
9 That beautiful statue is made . . . alabaster. (3,2)

DOWN

1 I'd like to insure my jewellery . . . theft and loss.
2 Only take these pills if you really feel . . . the weather.
3 . . . their bad start, the team were soon two goals ahead. (2,5,2)
6 The company changed the heating system . . . electricity to gas last year.
8 It's only made . . . glass, not diamonds.

KEY

SECTION ONE

1 1 a) on b) down c) up d) off e) up
to f) onto g) down h) down to

2 a = iii b = iv c = ii d = v
e = vi f = i

3 a) You'll be able to see the parade
better if you climb onto this wall.

b) The climber lost his hold, but
fortunately only slipped a few feet
down to the ledge.

c) The Rolling Stones' new single has
jumped up the charts.

d) Another tile has just fallen off the
roof.

e) I'm just going down the road to
get some milk.

f) The plant has climbed up to the
top of the window.

4 a) off b) down c) up to d) up
e) off f) on

2 1 a) along b) past c) along
d) through e) up and down
f) across g) past h) across

2 a = v b = i c = iii d = vi
e = iv f = ii

3 1 a) out of b) at c) for
d) down e) into f) towards

2 a) You need a visa to get into the
United States.

b) The brother and sister ran away
from summer camp.

c) I couldn't run for the bus because
my suitcase was so heavy.

d) I can't get out of this armchair.

e) The winner stepped onto stage.

f) The gun was aimed at the
president.

3 a) around b) into, to, towards, up to
c) into, onto

4 1 a) behind b) ahead of c) after
d) behind e) ahead of f) behind
g) after h) in front of

2 a = v b = i c = vi d = ii
e = iv f = iii

3 a) Baby ducks always swim close
behind their mother.

b) Your thinking is always one step
ahead of me.

c) Never walk behind a frightened
horse.

d) The police chased after the thief,
but lost him.

e) The winner was a few steps in
front of the others all the time.

f) People say that Leonardo da Vinci
was ahead of his time.

4 1 Gerald Ruskin 2 Roy Davies
3 Mandy Selby 4 Chris Pride
5 Andrew Jameson 6 Louise Mitchell

Consolidation

1 a) ahead of/in front of b) across,
behind c) up, down to d) out of
around, into, down to

6 ACROSS
1 behind 4 around 6 away from
8 across 9 through 10 onto 11 for
DOWN
2 into 3 down 4 ahead of
5 towards 7 out of

SECTION TWO

1 1 a) on top (of) b) above
c) beneath d) down/up e) under
f) above g) under (neath)/below
h) after

2 a) above/on top of
b) after/below c) below/on
d) above/on e) under f) on top
of/above/over g) over/on

3 a = i b = iv c) = v d = vi
e = iii f = ii

4 a) In chess, a bishop is ranked above
a knight.
b) Saudi Arabia is after the United
Arab Emirates in wealth.
c) I lived one floor below him.
d) The US national flag is always
flying over the American Embassy
building.
e) Your book is on (top of) your pen.
f) What he did is beneath contempt.
g) You'll find more fish down the
river.

5 1 Richardson 92%
2 Manson 79% 5 Herries 55%
3 Little 60% 6 Smith 39%
4 Fellowes 58% 7 Jones 10%

2 1 a) by b) at c) alongside
d) beside e) against f) on the left of
g) next to h) near

2 a) In the park b) No, it's next to the
restaurant c) At the station news
stand d) Next to the baker's e) It's
on the right of it f) No, on the left of
it

3 a) . . . the river/wall b) . . . the
station/ garage c) . . . the station
d) . . . the river e) . . . the chemist's

f) . . . of the bank g) . . . the
railway line h) . . . the river

4 on the right of, left of, next to, by,
along, next to, around, against, next
to, on the right of, near

3 1 a) opposite b)over c) across
d) before

2 a) facing b) in front of
c) over/across d) after e) behind
f) opposite g) before h) across

3 KEY
A Employment exchange
B Department store
C Travel agent's I Supermarket
D Boutique J Post office
E Bank K Record shop
F Dry cleaner's L Pet shop
G Patisserie M Doctor
H Cafe N Dentist

4 a = iv b = viii c = ii d = vi
e = vii f = i g = iii h = v

5 a) facing each other b) across/over
the river c) opposite d) behind/in
front of

Consolidation

1 a) around b) under c) against
d) near e) before f) opposite
g) along h) on top of

5 ACROSS
1 before 3 up 4 down 6 next to
8 at 9 near 13 behind
14 opposite 15 towards
DOWN
1 by 2 front 3 under 5 facing
7 on 10 against 11 below
12 around

SECTION THREE

1 1 a) on   b) within   c) around
   d) at   e) at   f) in   g) on/in   h) at
2 a) in, in   b) on, within   c) on, at, at
   d) on, in   e) on   f) within   g) at
4 a) . . .on 1 January   b) . . . at 9.20
   c) . . . at 9.00
5 I'd like to visit you at Easter. The
   plane arrives on Saturday at 6.30
   p.m. Please cable if this is OK.
   Sorry, we're not at home in April.
   We're free around the end of March.
   Can you come on the 25th or 26th?

2 1 a) by   b) after   c) past   d) to
   e) after   f) by   g) after
2 a) It's quarter past one.
   b) I must pay the deposit by
      Saturday.
   c) The concert begins at quarter to
      eleven and finishes at half-past
      twelve.
   d) The train left at ten to eleven, but
      unfortunately I got to the station
      at five past eleven.
   e) She'll see you after work.
   f) You must arrive before ten-thirty.
3 a = iv past   b = viii to, in   c = v
   past, in   d = ii to   e = iii past
   f = vi after   g = i to
   h = vii past, in
4 8.55 BC218 Edinburgh
   9.25 BA4242 Miami
   10.10 AF103 Paris CDG
   10.10 PA2190 Dallas
   10.20 SAS202 Stockholm
   10.15 PA1918 New York

3 1 a) during   b) from, to
   c) through/for   d) for   e) about

   f) as from   g) since   h) in (side)
   i) within
2 a = vi   b = iv   c = iii   d = i
   e = ii   f = v
3 a) I will have to go to school until
      I'm sixteen.
   b) He stayed in China for two years.
   c) Report to the welfare officer
      between one and five p.m.
   d) Inflation has risen during the past
      few years.
   e) They've been in power for about
      two years.
   f) I haven't been there since my
      childhood.
4 a) Because of a serious accident Elena
      was unable to walk from eight to
      13.
   b) Martin has been living in Holland
      for six years.
   c) African children spend about six
      years in full-time education.
   d) He proposed to his fiancee during
      a Mediterranean cruise.
   e) As from tomorrow I'll give up
      drinking.
   f) He was in prison throughout 1967.

Consolidation
1 a = v   b = ii   c = vi   d = i
   e = iii   f = vii   g = iv
2 a) No, not the weekend
   b) After 15 May, 1983
   c) In an hour and 38 minutes
   d) It's at 6.28
   e) At 7.40
   f) About two hours
   g) About three and a half hours

3 at, by, 6.50, until, at, 13.03, by, in,
   16.22/16.52, to/past, by, 18.30, for,
   two, during
5 ACROSS
   1 up   4 inside   6 at   7 from

9 since   10 for   11 after

DOWN
2 past   3 within   5 during
8 before

SECTION FOUR

1 1 a) from   b) owing to/due to   c) for
      d) through   e) with   f) out of   g) of
      h) because of/due to
   2 a) He lives for his family.
      b) I am not trembling with fear, but
          anger.
      c) He went abroad because of the
          unemployment situation.
      d) His tongue swelled from lack of
          water.
      e) You were not paid due to
          computer error.
      f) I joined this society out of concern
          for handicapped people.
      g) Owing to lack of interest the
          lecture has been cancelled.
      h) The fight was started through a
          regrettable misunderstanding.
2 1 a) by   b) via   c) by   d) by means of
      e) by, with   ) by   g) with
      h) by means of
   2 a = v   b = vi   c = vii   d = i
      e = iii   f = ii   g = viii   h = iv
   3 a) with a knife   b) by ship/boat
      c) by means of the window   d) via
      Dover and Calais   e) by
      telegram/telex   f) with a cleaner
   4 a) Green is made by mixing yellow
          and blue.
      b) German politicians are elected by
          (means of) proportional repre-
          sentation.
      c) I always make clothes by hand.
      d) Parcels should be tied with string.

      e) The Prime Minister travelled to
          Australia via Singapore.
      f) All the dresses were designed by
          Yves St. Laurent.
      g) The refugee left the country by
          means of a false passport.
      h) You can go by road or by air to
          Moscow, but not by sea.
3 1 a) with   b) like   c) by   d) with
      e) as
   2 a) like   b) like   c) as   d) as, as
   3 a) The teacher says there isn't much
          improvement in her work, but
          she's getting better little by little.
      b) Alcohol makes some people act
          like fools.
      c) Watches are made with precision.
      d) I won't be able to write/speak
          about these plans with conviction,
          as I don't . . .
      e) As a doctor/nurse, I advise you
          to . . .
      f) The apple tree is growing little by
          little/by the year.
4 1 a) for   b) for   c) towards   d) for
      e) for   f) in
   2 a) . . . for listening to music
      b) . . . for digging
      c) . . . for holding down papers
      d) . . . for cutting
      e) . . . for telling the time
      f) . . . for drinking out of
      g) . . . for writing
      h) . . . for putting flowers in

3 a-for-iv b-in-v c-in-i
d-for-vi e-in-ii f-in-iii

Consolidation

1 a) because of/through/due to
b) through   c) towards/for   d) with
e) like   f) for   g) via   h) through
i) as   j) from   k) by/with   l) owing
to/because of   m) by   n) with
2 a) the door   b) money/revenge
c) an attacker   d) a scarf
e) the window   f) motor bike

3 . . . for money, . . . jealousy, . . . a
key, . . . the door, . . . knife/blunt
object, . . . scarf, . . . the fall/ hitting
it on the floor, . . . a journey/
travelling, . . . via
6 ACROSS
1 for   3 by   4 via   6 in
7 through   9 towards   11 like
12 of
DOWN
2 owing to   3 because of
5 with   8 as   10 out of

SECTION FIVE

1 1 a) at b) about c) around d) near
e) in f) about g) by h) about
3 a = vii b = iii c = i d = v
e = ix f = ii g = iv h = viii
i = vi
4 a) around b) near c) about d) by,
at e) about f) near
5 a) Versailles is near Paris.
b) The Colisseum is in Rome.
c) The Alps are in/around
Switzerland.
d) The Crown Jewels are kept in the
Tower of London.
e) Australia is near New Zealand.
f) There are mines around the north
of England.

2 1 a) over b) against c) between
d) like e) below/under f) beside
g) up to h) after
2 a) How tall are you?
b) Are you like your father?
c) Is (Notre Dame) a beautiful church?
d) How old do you have to be to
vote?
e) Was his work up to the usual
standard?
f) Is this (bag) leather?

g) What's the temperature?
h) Are you like your (sister)?
3 a) Can you tell the difference
between margarine and butter?
b) You can't vote if you're under
eighteen.
c) The class can't take over twelve
people.
d) That instrument sounds like a
guitar.
e) Won't red clash against an orange
background?
f) Her husband doesn't come near
her in stupidity.
g) I don't think she's up to the
standard of my class.

3 1 a) in addition to, plus
b) in addition to c) plus d) plus
e) minus f) plus, times
g) besides h) divided by
2 a = v b = iii c = iv d = i
e = ii

Consolidation

1 a) between b) around c) after
d) plus e) over f) on/around
g) against h) below i) times
j) plus

2 a) What are the differences between a hotel and an inn?
 b) How many hotels are near here?
 c) Where's the motel?
 d) How many hotels are there in the village?
 e) What's Ethel' Guest House like?
 f) How many bed does the motel have?
 g) Are many of the hotels big?/Do many of the hotels have over 200 beds?
 h) What's Ethel's Guest House like?

6 ACROSS
1 unlike 3 up to 7 against
9 over 10 near 11 under 12 by
14 together with 15 near 16 in
17 plus 18 minus

DOWN
2 near 4 over 5 about 6 at
8 in addition to 11 up
12 besides 13 between

SECTION SIX

1 1 a) in favour of b) for the sake of
 c) contrary to d) against
 e) opposite to f) for g) for
 h) behind/against/in favour of
 2 a = ii b = iv c = iii d = v
 e = i
 3 a) The International Monetary Fund is behind the government's plan to revive the steel industry.
 b) I'm all for having a party as soon as possible.
 c) The (new) football team are behind his (new) ideas.
 d) Are you in favour of Women's Liberation?
 e) There's a law against drinking and driving.
 4 a) All his beliefs are contrary to mine.
 b) I'm for restructuring the company.
 c) I'm against siting Cruise missiles in Europe.
 d) Are you in favour of his plans for a secret ballot?
 e) My father is behind my brother's business.

2 1 a) among b) between c) in
 d) inside e) outside/beyond
 f) within/inside g) between
 h) among
 2 a) in b) under c) of d) out of
 e) among f) around g) outside
 h) under
 3 a) among, inside b) in, among
 c) between d) in, among, around
 e) between
 4 a) I was between two policemen.
 b) You don't think about me when I'm out of sight.
 c) Those two seem to have an invisible wall around them.
 d) I think 'The Tempest' is among Shakespeare's best plays.
 e) Some people never go outside their own experiences.
 f) I'm sorry, but I think your brother is beyond hope now.
 g) If you want to find their phone number, look under his name, not hers.
 h) The person we're looking for is inside this house.

3 1 a) apart from/except (for) b) apart from/except (for) c) but/except (for) d) barring e) except (for) f) but

2 a = iv b = iii c = vi d = v
e = i f = ii
Exceptions:
a) Coca-Cola b) turquoise
c) Maradona d) India e) New York

4 1 a) for b) over c) for d) on
e) as for f) after

2 a = vi b = iii c = viii d = ii
e = vii f = iv g = v h = i

3 The incorrect ones are:
a) a good film b) oriental philosophers c) your health
d) exams e) your friends
f) a journal

5 2 a) on b) away from c) with
d) without e) out of f) on

3 a) behind b) to c) on d) of
e) of f) from, from g) off, of
h) behind

4 a) Which country did Karl Marx come from?
b) Do you take tea with or without sugar?
c) How far away from the USA is the USSR?
d) On which animal do you find a mane?
e) Does the national flag of Japan have a moon on it?
f) Which island is off the south coast of India?

5 a) He came from Germany.

b) (depends on students)
c) The USA is about 50 km away from the USSR.
d) You find a mane on a horse.
e) Yes, the national flag of Japan has a moon on it.
f) Sri Lanka is off the south coast of India.

Consolidation

1 beyond, of, of, from, to, between, against, in favour of, between, away from, for, for, without, contrary to, without/beyond, except (for), as for, among, under

2 a) . . . 'Ghandi' b). . . Mahatma Ghandi c). . . his life d). . . fear, poverty and hatred e) . . . prejudice f). . . his country g) . . . Muslims and Hindus h). . . peace

3 from — to inside — outside within — without against — for in favour of — against off — on

5 a) behind = for b) as for = as to
c) beyond = outside d) off = away from e) except for = apart from

6 ACROSS
1 in favour of 6 opposite 8 beside
9 away 12 as for 13 inside
15 around 17 contrary 19 without
DOWN
1 in support 2 for the sake of
3 out 4 from 5 outside
7 over 8 beyond 10 after
11 with 13 in 14 except
15 among 16 under 18 as to

SECTION SEVEN

1 1 a) in   b) with   c) for   d) under
   e) by   f) with   g) in   h) for
   2 a = iv   b = viii   c = i/vii
     d = vi   e = vii/i   f = ii   g = v
     h = iii
   3 a) by   b) in   c) under   d) for   e) in
     f) for   g) in   h) with
   4 a) This town can be dangerous by
       night.
     b) We have to sleep with mosquito
        nets here.
     c) The document was sent under
        separate cover.
     d) He lost his passport in his
        carelessness.
     e) This taxi service is only for
        disabled people.
     f) He's in a bad mood.
     g) The car will only start with the
        choke.
     h) People look younger by soft
        lighting.
2 1 a) despite/in spite of   b) for all
     c) despite/in spite of/for all   d) for
     all   e) despite/in spite of
     f) despite/in spite of
   2 a) Despite/in spite of/for all his
        kindness . . .
     b) Despite/in spite of the heavy
        rain . . .
     c) Despite/in spite of using . . .
     d) Despite/in spite of his wife's death
        in a fall . . .
     e) Despite/in spite of the failure
        of . . .
     f) Despite/in spite of the change of
        government . . .
3 1 a) of   b) with   c) with   d) in
     e) of   f) out of   g) from

   h) of/out of
   2 a — platinum   b — cream
     c — felt   d — bristle and plastic
     e — watercolour
   3 a) . . . of marble   b). . . in oil
     c). . . of eggs   d) . . . of bricks
     e) . . . of glass   f) . . . with lead
     g) . . . with eggs and oil
     h) . . . of gold
4 1 of, with, of, with
   2 from, with, with
   3 with, from, with, with, with
4 1 a) into   b) for   c) against   d) into
     e) to   f) into   g) for   h) into
   2 a) into   b) for   c) against
     d) from, to   e) against   f) for
     g) into   h) from, to
   3 a) into   b) into   c) from . . . to
     d) against   e) for   f) to

Consolidation

   1 a) with   b) for   c) in spite of
     d) in   e) into   f) under   g) for
     h) for   i) for all   j) of
   2 a = iii   b = vi   c = v   d = ii
     e = i   f = iv
   3 a) Fabian continued drinking, in spite
        of the doctor telling him not to.
     b) Could you lend me £30 against my
        watch as security?
     c) Ronald Reagan went from being
        an actor to the President of the
        USA.
     d) Our cakes are made from the
        finest ingredients.
     e) I'm in a difficult situation.
     f) The puppy grew into a dog within
        a couple of months.
     g) This kind of comedy is for
        children.

h) Despite the cold winter the rose
bush bloomed the next summer.
i) This jumper is made of pure new
wool.
j) I'm taking this dress back to the
shop to change it for a larger size.
4 a) under   b) with   c) in
d) with   e) by   f) of   g) for

h) under

6 ACROSS
4 in   5 despite   6 for   7 to
9 out of
DOWN
1 against   2 under   3 in spite of
6 from   8 of

INDEX

The prepositions here are classified according to the section in which they appear (S) and page number.